BORDER

PLANTS

BORDER
PLANTS

ALAN TOOGOOD

WARD LOCK LIMITED · LONDON

© Ward Lock Limited 1987

First published in Great Britain in 1987
by Ward Lock Limited, 8 Clifford
Street, London W1X 1RB
An Egmont Company

House editor Denis Ingram

Text filmset in Bembo by
Paul Hicks Limited
Middleton, Manchester

Printed in Portugal

British Library Cataloguing in Publication Data
Border plants.
  1. Garden borders
  I. Toogood, Alan R.
  635.9'63   SB424

  ISBN 0–7063–6502–X

Frontispiece: This attractive frontage to a Surrey cottage has shrubs spilling over a mellow brick wall with campanulas and valerian at its foot.

CONTENTS

ACKNOWLEDGEMENTS

All the colour photographs in this book were taken by Bob Challinor, and all the line drawings were drawn by Rosemary Wise.

The publishers are grateful to the following persons for allowing their gardens to photographed: Mrs A.M. Sitwell (pp 10 & 15); Mr & Mrs G Bunting (p 26); Mr & Mrs J Morris (pp 31 & 35); Mr & Mrs A.E. Pedder (pp 42 & 43); Beth Chatto (pp 47, 50, 55 & 58); Sheila Macqueen (p 63); Mr & Mrs R Raworth (p 71 (left)); Miss H O'Kelly & Miss B Harper (p 71 (right)); Mr & Mrs P Hickman (p 78); Mr & Mrs W May (p 83); and Rev. & Mrs R.B. Feast (p 91).

PUBLISHER'S NOTE

Readers are requested to note that in order to make the text intelligible in both hemispheres, plant flowering times, etc. are generally described in terms of seasons, not months. The following table provides an approximate 'translation' of seasons into months for the two hemispheres.

NORTHERN HEMISPHERE				SOUTHERN HEMISPHERE
Mid-winter	=	January	=	Mid-summer
Late winter	=	February	=	Late summer
Early spring	=	March	=	Early autumn
Mid-spring	=	April	=	Mid-autumn
Late spring	=	May	=	Late autumn
Early Summer	=	June	=	Early winter
Mid-summer	=	July	=	Mid-winter
Late summer	=	August	=	Late winter
Early autumn	=	September	=	Early spring
Mid-autumn	=	October	=	Mid-spring
Late autumn	=	November	=	Late spring
Early winter	=	December	=	Early summer

Measurements are generally cited in metric followed by the imperial equivalent in parentheses. In a few instances, owing to pressure on space, the imperial equivalent has been omitted.

CHAPTER 1

PAST AND PRESENT

Border plants are perennial; that is, they live for many years and are considered permanent occupants of the garden. They can be divided into two distinct groups, the first being the herbaceous perennials. All the top growth of herbaceous plants (the stems and foliage) dies right down to ground level in the autumn, when it is cut off and discarded. The plants overwinter as dormant crowns consisting of growth buds and roots. In the spring these buds start into growth, producing new stems and leaves and, of course, flowers.

The second group contains the evergreen perennials; in other words, plants which retain their leaves all the year round. A well-known example is bergenia. The evergreens are in the minority as most perennial border plants are herbaceous in habit.

The majority of border plants are grown for their flowers but some, such as the hostas or plantain lilies, for their attractive foliage.

The majority of border plants are very hardy, surviving even severe winters, but some are on the tender side and may succumb to severe Arctic spells as they originate from warmer climates than ours. So from what parts of the world do perennials originate?

From North America we have many, such as asters or Michaelmas daisies, lupins, border phloxes and solidago or golden rod. The zauschnerias or Californian fuchsias come from California and Mexico and so are a bit on the tender side.

From Europe we have several perennials including irises (south-east Europe), hardy geraniums (Pyrenees, Alps, etc) and veronicas.

A lot of the plants we grow originate from Asia, like delphiniums (Siberia, so they should be hardy), *Papaver orientale*, the oriental poppy (Asia), hostas or plantain lilies (Japan and China), meconopsis or blue poppies (Himalayas), *Paeonia lactiflora* (Siberia) and primulas like the candelabra species (China, Japan and the Himalayas).

On the tender side are the phormiums or New Zealand flax and the agapanthus or African lilies from South Africa.

Many of the border plants we grow are the original species or wild plants but others are hybrids, crosses between species, the work of plant breeders and nurserymen. Plant breeding has, over the years, been particularly intense among the popular border plants like asters or Michaelmas daisies, irises, lupins, delphiniums, phlox and solidago.

But how has plant breeding improved border plants? Well, many are now dwarfer and self-supporting so they do not need to be provided with supports. Others have a more restrained habit of growth – in other words, they do not spread through a border like weeds – a notable example being the golden rod or solidago. Once upon a time this perennial was barred from many gardens because it was so rampant. But not any longer. It is also possible to buy dwarf varieties of golden rod, which is naturally a very tall plant.

Size of flowers or flower spikes has been greatly increased in some perennials, notably the delphiniums and lupins. The modern hybrids are far removed from the wild species. Many of the hybrid perennials also have a much longer flowering season than the wild species, making them more worthy of garden space.

Many hybrids have a much wider colour range than is found in species. Again one can quote lupins, which are available in virtually every colour. Delphiniums come in many more colours than the original blue, including pink and red. Irises come in almost every colour, new varieties appearing on the market each year.

Breeders have gone to town on some foliage perennials, too, especially the hostas or plantain lilies. A lot of the work has been done in the U.S.A. and many American varieties are now available in Britain. There are lots of golden, variegated and 'blue' hostas to choose from now, instead of just plain green foliage.

Perennials have been grown in gardens for hundreds of years, but not always for decorative purposes. In the past, particularly in medieval times, some were used as medicinal herbs or for culinary purposes.

In the last century and the early part of this century perennials were widely grown in their own special borders for decorative effect, these being known as herbaceous borders. Very often there were double borders, with a wide grass path between, each border being backed by a tall formal hedge. The plants available at that time were often tall, necessitating supports for most. These borders were quite labour-intensive and they went out of fashion.

Perennials were also very much a part of nineteenth-century cottage gardens, being mixed liberally with other kinds of plants like shrubs and even with fruits and vegetables. The traditional cottage garden is coming back into fashion and there is currently great interest in the old-fashioned perennials.

But what about modern uses of perennials? With the introduction over the years of many labour-saving plants (plants which do not need supports) there is a revival of interest in the herbaceous border.

Labour-saving perennials are also widely planted in their own special beds set in, say, lawns and these are known as island beds.

In small gardens, though, there is not the space available to devote an entire border or bed to one type of plant and so mixed borders are commonly encountered in modern pocket-handkerchief gardens – borders containing all sorts of plants like shrubs, perennials, bulbs and annuals.

Owners of larger gardens, particularly, are often concerned with making their gardens as labour saving as possible and so ground-cover plants are in vogue – plants that form dense mats or carpets of growth which effectively suppress annual weeds. There is a number of perennials which are ideal for ground cover.

People are becoming more educated in the uses of plants and choose plants to suit particular conditions in a garden. So there is a lot of interest in plants suited to, say, hot dry areas, to shady places, to clay soils and so on.

A lot of people are becoming far more adventurous in their choice of plants, quickly tiring of the limited ranges in garden centres. There is great interest in the more unusual plants, which are not necessarily any more difficult to grow than common plants. In recent years we have seen the setting up of several nurseries specializing in unusual perennials and other hardy plants.

Conservation is uppermost in many gardeners' minds and there is considerable interest in preserving the old varieties of perennials and indeed of many other plants. The National Council for the Conservation of Plants and Gardens, which is based at the Royal Horticultural Society's garden at Wisley, in Surrey, is responsible for organizing national collections of plants, many including perennials, to ensure they are not lost. The current interest in cottage gardening should also help to ensure that many of the delightful old-fashioned varieties continue to remain in cultivation.

All of the ways of growing and using perennial border plants mentioned above are covered in detail in the following chapters, together with advice on their cultivation and propagation.

Over 200 kinds of perennials are described, which is a very wide range indeed. There are plants to suit every part of a garden and all kinds of conditions and climates. So I hope you will stock your garden with a good selection. After all, perennial border plants are as important as shrubs and roses: no garden is complete without them.

This border's fascination stems from its richly varied planting and the skilful gradation from carpeting plants at the front to delphiniums and climbing roses at the back.

CHAPTER 2

PREPARATIONS

CHOOSING A SITE

If border plants are to grow and flower well they must be provided with optimum conditions. For the vast majority this means a border or bed which receives sun for much of the day, such as a south- or west-facing aspect. If sun-loving plants are grown in shade they will make weak, spindly growth and produce few if any flowers.

There are exceptions, though. Some border plants, discussed in Chapter 8, thrive in shade. Conversely, if you have an exceptionally hot dry spot (perhaps too extreme for the majority of border plants) you will also find a range of plants which relish these conditions – see Chapter 9. As you can see, then, it is a case of choosing plants to suit the site.

The sun-loving border plants like an open situation, one that is not overshadowed by trees. But on the other hand the bed or border should, ideally, be well sheltered from the wind. This is particularly important for tall perennials and those with thin stems, for wind can flatten them, especially when they are heavy with rain. Of course, the plants can be provided with supports, but far more in the way of supports will be needed in a windy spot. In a sheltered site many perennials will not need supports, thus saving you time, expense and energy. Hedges, taller screens, groups of shrubs, etc, will all help to create sheltered conditions.

If your garden is really exposed, and there is little you can do to tame the wind, then grow the really dwarf and prostrate kinds of border plants, including the wide range of alpines or rock plants. Height in your planting schemes can then be provided by wind-resistant shrubs, conifers and other plants.

BACKGROUNDS

A conventional border needs some kind of background. Very often this is provided by the garden boundary. Evergreen hedges are a good choice, for they are effective all the year round and one does not have the problem of clearing up fallen leaves in the autumn – not easy among border plants.

A variety of the cherry laurel, *Prunus laurocerasus* 'Rotundifolia', makes a good hedge with its large rounded leaves. Yew, *Taxus baccata*, is slower growing but makes a really dense hedge. There are several conifers, too, like a variety of Lawson cypress, *Chamaecyparis lawsoniana* 'Green Hedger', and the western red cedar, *Thuja plicata*. Although it makes a good hedge, I would not recommend holly (unless it is one of the non-prickly kinds like *Ilex* × *altaclarensis* 'Camelliifolia'), as the fallen leaves make hand weeding a misery!

The colour of all these hedging plants is deepish or rich green – flowering plants show up well with such a background.

Island beds, perhaps set in a lawn, do not have a background immediately behind them, but in the distance there needs to be something fairly 'solid' so that the beds show to advantage. Perhaps bold groups of foliage shrubs or conifers, in various shades of green (not gold or other colours).

Close-boarded fencing, including woven or lapped fencing panels, makes a good background for a border – generally it is used as a boundary for the garden. If it is treated with a dark oak horticultural wood preservative the plants would show up really well. Wattle fencing panels would make a good background in a country garden.

Brick walls are suitable backgrounds, or perhaps a stone wall – maybe a dry-stone wall in a country garden.

Walls and fences can, of course, be clothed with climbing plants. In a herbaceous border you could use annual climbers, like sweet peas, climbing nasturtiums, canary creeper (*Tropaeolum peregrinum*) and morning glory (*Ipomoea*).

In a mixed border permanent climbers and wall shrubs could be used, such as evergreen ceanothus, climbing and rambler roses, clematis, ivies, jasmines, honeysuckles and pyracanthas.

SOILS

Border plants are very adaptable and grow well in a wide range of soils, whether they are acid (free from lime or chalk) or alkaline (limey or chalky). Soils may be basically sandy, loam or clay – all are suitable provided any necessary improvement is carried out. Whatever the type of soil in your garden, it must be well drained, and not become waterlogged or very wet and sticky in the autumn and winter. Wet soil is fatal to the great majority of border plants. Some border plants require *moist* soil, which does not dry out in summer, but even so it must not lie very wet in winter (see Chapters 8 and 10). Other border plants will thrive in soils which dry out considerably in summer (see Chapters 8 and 9).

SOIL PREPARATION

The very first step in preparing a bed or border is to eradicate perennial weeds, like ground elder, bindweed, nettles, couch grass, etc. During the growing season – spring and summer – the weeds should be sprayed with a suitable weedkiller, used according to the manufacturer's instructions. For broad-leaved weeds (like ground elder) use glyphosate. For grasses (like couch) use alloxydim sodium.

If used correctly, the weeds should be dead by the autumn, when digging can commence. I recommend double digging, to two depths of the spade, when preparing beds and borders, as this helps to improve drainage. To double dig a bed or border you start at one end and work to the other end. First take out a trench right across one end, 60 cm (24 in) wide and the depth of the spade. Deposit the soil at the other end, as it will be used to fill the final trench.

Then get into the trench and dig the bottom to the depth of the spade (or use a fork if the ground is hard). There is no need to turn the soil over.

Next take out another 60 cm (24 in) wide trench immediately behind the first, throwing the soil forward, and turning it over, into the first trench. Again dig the bottom of the trench. Continue in this way, and when you reach the end of the bed or border fill the last trench with the soil from the first one.

During digging you should remove roots of perennial weeds, even though they were killed with weedkiller. Also chop through and remove any tree roots. As mentioned earlier, the majority of border plants like an open spot, well away from trees, so roots should not be a problem. Tree roots take a lot of moisture from the soil in the growing season and so most border plants will suffer. If, however, you are preparing soil beneath trees for shade-loving plants (see Chapter 8) then ignore tree roots, and dig the soil as best you can.

During digging bulky organic matter should be added to each trench. This improves all soils, whether sandy or gravelly types, chalk soils or heavy clays, for it not only helps to improve drainage of heavy types, but also helps to conserve moisture during dry weather in naturally well-drained soils. Suitable organic matter is well-rotted farmyard manure, garden compost, spent hops, spent mushroom compost, shredded bark and peat. Spread a layer over the bottom of each trench after digging it. As a rough guide, a quarter of a barrowload will be sufficient for each 1.2 m (4 ft) length of trench. If you have a very dry soil, it would be a good idea to mix organic matter into the top 30 cm (12 in) as well.

If your soil is badly drained, inclined to lie very wet and sticky over winter, you are strongly advised to incorporate grit or coarse horticultural sand as well during digging. Add a layer to each trench. If you are able to buy sufficient, it would be a good idea also to mix some into the lower soil and into the top 30 cm (12 in). Then the soil would be well opened up to two depths of the spade, considerably improving

Note the generous planting here which really fills the border, and its sweeping curve set off by a healthy rich green lawn.

drainage. You will find it cheaper to buy grit or coarse sand in bulk — by the cubic metre.

After digging, the bed or border is left over winter for the weather to work on it. Then in early spring it is finally prepared for planting. Apply a base dressing of general-purpose fertilizer. Break the soil down with a fork and then firm it by treading over the bed systematically, with the weight on your heels.

Finally fork lightly over the bed again to create a loose tilth on the surface for planting, and carry out any final levelling that may be needed. Now all is ready for planting.

SHAPES OF BORDERS

The shape of a border or bed should be in keeping with the style of the garden. In most gardens the shape of the lawn will dictate the shape of the surrounding borders.

FORMAL
In a formal garden the lawn is generally square or rectangular and therefore the surrounding borders will be of formal shape — also generally rectangular. I would urge you to avoid having very narrow borders as these are difficult to plant effectively. If lack of space is a problem, it would be better to have fewer borders and to make them reasonably wide. A good width for a border is 2.7–3.6 m (9–12 ft).

If you are contemplating island beds in a lawn, then these can be formal shapes, too, such as circular, square, triangular, etc.

INFORMAL
Informality is the trend today in garden design — getting away from straight lines. I would go so far as to say that informality is the best choice for small gardens, as it can create the illusion of more space. Of course, it is essential in country or cottage gardens.

How we can achieve this effect? Take a small town garden, for instance, and instead of creating a square or rectangular lawn in the middle, give the lawn sweeping or gently curving edges. This will, of course, result in surrounding borders of informal shapes; they, too, will have irregular, curving edges.

If you decide to have a group of island beds in the lawn, then give them also gently curving edges.

On the practical side, shapes of beds or borders are very easily marked out with a length of hosepipe or rope laid on the ground. This can be rearranged and adjusted until you are satisfied with the shape.

CHAPTER 3

PLANTING

BUYING PLANTS

Border plants can be bought in containers from garden centres, either in pots or flexible polythene bags. They can, if desired, be bought when they are in flower, so that you can see exactly what you are buying. All the popular border plants are offered by garden centres, but there is not a wide choice of varieities.

In the spring some chain stores offer border plants – these are pre-packed, with their roots well wrapped in peat and polythene. Make sure the top growth of these plants is not too advanced when buying – it is all right if the buds are just starting into growth. Again, only the most popular kinds are offered.

If you want to buy a wider range of plants than the garden centres and chain stores offer, and you desire a wide choice of varieties, then buy mail-order from a perennial-plant specialist, such as Bressingham Gardens (see Appendix for address). Plants are dispatched in autumn or spring.

TIME TO PLANT

Border plants can be planted in early- or mid-spring, as then they establish quickly, because the soil is warming up and becoming drier. Container-grown plants can be planted in summer, too. I know that some books recommend autumn planting, but this can only be safely done if the soil is very well drained. If it is prone to lying wet and cold over winter there is a great risk of young plants succumbing to root rot. If you have a light sandy or gravelly soil, for instance, then autumn planting is certainly safe, but I would not recommend it if the soil is mostly clay or otherwise 'heavy'.

METHODS OF PLANTING

Let's first consider planting border plants (Fig. 1) which are supplied in containers, from a garden centre.

First make sure the compost is thoroughly moist, by watering if necessary the evening before. Then for each plant take out a hole with a spade. It should be slightly wider than the soilball of the plant, and of such a depth that after planting the top of the soilball is only about 12 mm (½ in) below the surface of the surrounding soil.

Next carefully remove the plant from its container. If it is in a flexible polythene bag slit the bag with a knife down one side and underneath and peel away the polythene. If the plant is in a rigid pot, invert it, tap the rim of the pot on a solid object of some kind (such as the spade handle) and slide off the pot. The objective with container-grown plants is to disturb the soilball as little as possible when planting. This is particularly important if the plants are in full growth.

Next place the plant in the centre of the hole, then fill in the space all round with fine soil, firming well by treading with your heels as you proceed.

Fig. 1 When planting a containerised border plant, carefully remove the container (*a*) so as not to disturb the roots, work fine soil all round the rootball (*b*), firm in well and then remove footprints (*c*).

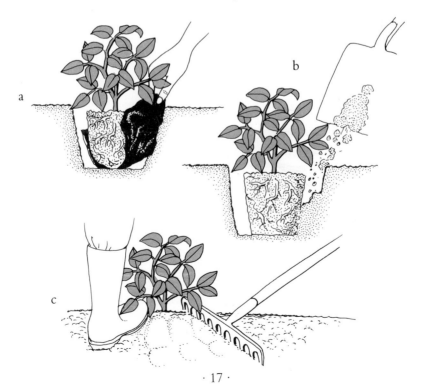

Fig. 2 For bare-root plants, make sure the hole is deep enough to allow the roots to dangle straight down (*a*). Work fine soil between them (*b*), then firm it thoroughly (*c*).

For plants which do not have a soilball around their roots, such as pre-packed plants, root-wrapped plants from a mail-order supplier, and your own divisions (see Lifting and Dividing in Chapter 4), make a hole for each which is deep enough to allow the roots to dangle straight down to their full length. If the hole is too shallow the roots will turn upwards and then the plant will not establish too well (Fig. 2). Also bear in mind when planting that the crown of the plant (that is, where the dormant buds are situated) should be level with the surrounding soil after planting. In other words, the buds should not be covered with soil.

When you are satisfied that the plant is positioned correctly in its hole, return fine soil around the roots, at the same time firming it thoroughly, either with your hands or by treading all round with your heels.

When you have completed planting lightly prick over the soil surface with a fork to remove footprints and to relieve surface compaction.

PLANTING IN GROUPS

In Chapters 5 to 9 you will see that I recommend planting border plants in groups of each kind to create impact. Single plants have far less impact and create a 'spotty' effect in a bed or border. But how large should these groups be? It does, of course, depend on the width of the border, but for borders of average width – 2.7–3.6 m (9–12 ft) – I suggest groups of about 1 sq m (or 1 sq yd). Such an area will take several plants of most perennials. Refer to the Appendix for number of plants per sq m (or sq yd).

Of course, when planting a bed or border you must take account of heights of plants. It's no good planting a tall plant in front of a short one, for instance. In a border backed by a hedge, fence or wall the rule is to plant the taller subjects at the back and to grade down to the front with shorter plants. In a bed which can be viewed from all sides plant the tallest kinds in the centre and grade down to the edges all round with shorter subjects. However, as you will see later, I do not stick too rigidly to these rules, otherwise the effect is too regimented. More details of grouping plants for effective display are given in Chapters 5 to 9 inclusive.

A word of advice when planting a border backed by a hedge, fence or wall. Leave a space of at least 90 cm (3 ft) between the backing and the rear row of plants. The soil can become very dry near to a hedge, fence or wall, and in those conditions most border plants will suffer from lack of moisture and make very poor growth – unless, of course, you are prepared to water heavily whenever necessary. But this is not the only reason why you should not plant hard up against a background. By leaving a space you will ensure better air circulation around the plants. Consequently growth will be better, and the plants will be less prone to attacks by diseases such as mildew and grey mould (botrytis). So it's worth making a border 90 cm (3 ft) wider than really needed, to allow for this space at the back.

Having said all this, I should say that I do grow climbing plants and wall shrubs against walls and fences. But even with these I always leave a slight space between the plants and the support to allow for air circulation, and pay particular attention to watering, especially for the first few years after planting, until the plants are really well established.

CHAPTER 4

CARE AND INCREASE

Border plants should not be neglected after planting or most of them will soon deteriorate and flowering will be poor. Regular tasks such as feeding, watering and weeding will keep the plants growing well, and regular division will ensure young vigorous plants.

FEEDING

In mid- or late spring each year give your border plants a topdressing of general-purpose fertilizer such as Growmore, or a flower-garden fertilizer. Apply about 140 g per sq m (4 oz per sq yd) and lightly fork or hoe it into the surface.

Feeding is best carried out on weed-free, moist soil, and before mulching.

If, in the summer, growth seems to be poor you can give it a boost by applying a foliar feed. Basically this is a liquid fertilizer which is diluted with water and sprayed on to the leaves of the plants, where it is quickly absorbed. There are several proprietary foliar fertilizers available. Foliar feeding should not be used as a substitute for the spring topdressing.

WATERING

The soil should not be allowed to dry out during the spring and summer or the plants will make poor growth. The aim should be to keep the top 15 cm (6 in) moist, and this means applying water when the top 2.5 cm (1 in) of the soil surface starts to become dry.

You should apply enough water for it to penetrate at least 15 cm (6 in) deep, and this means the equivalent of 2.5 cm (1 in) of rain. This amounts to about 27 litres of water per sq m (4¾ gallons per sq yd). Obviously you will find it too time-consuming applying this amount of water by hand, so use a gentle sprinkler attached to a hosepipe. You can measure the amount of water being applied by standing a few empty tins over the border. When these have 2.5 cm of water in the bottom you know you have watered sufficiently.

Nevertheless it is a good idea to check the depth of penetration about an hour after watering, by digging a test hole 15 cm (6 in) deep with a hand trowel. If the soil is moist at the bottom you know you have applied sufficient water.

Newly planted border plants are especially susceptible to dry conditions so keep these well watered. Even plants which revel in hot dry conditions (see Chapter 9) will make better growth if they are watered during drought conditions. Of course, there may be restrictions on the use of water during a drought, but if you use a mulch soil moisture will be conserved to some extent.

WEED CONTROL

Dense weed growth around border plants will seriously retard their growth, so keep on top of weeds at all times. I have already mentioned that you should plant only in a weed-free border – free from perennial weeds. So, hopefully, you will only be troubled by annual weeds, which grow in astronomical numbers from seeds.

Fig. 3 A 'spot weeder' containing glyphosate will control the odd perennial weed growing among border plants.

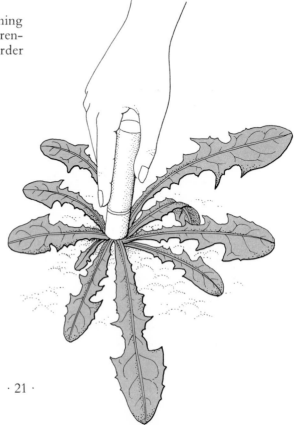

However, if one or two perennial weeds do appear among border plants they should either be carefully dug out, including roots, with a border fork, or treated with one of the 'spot weeders' containing glyphosate weedkiller (Fig. 3). If the weed is growing in the centre of a border plant then that plant will have to be lifted in the autumn or early spring and the weed extricated.

Control of annual weeds can be by various means. Regular hoeing when the weather is dry, and when the weeds are in the seedling stage, is the traditional method. If you allow the weeds to become large (not recommended) then hand pulling will have to be resorted to, first loosening the soil with a border fork – time-consuming and laborious work.

It is possible to keep the soil free from annual weeds by using a weedkiller containing propachlor. This prevents the germination of weed seeds and the effect can last for up to eight weeks after application. Propachlor will not harm border plants. It is supplied as granules in a shaker pack and is sprinkled evenly over the soil, which must be moist and free from weeds. Follow the manufacturer's instructions on use. After application the soil must not be disturbed.

If you use a mulch you will not have to carry out hoeing nor apply weedkiller as it will suppress the growth of annual weeds.

MULCHING

This involves completely covering the soil between plants with either organic or inorganic material, the purpose being to suppress the growth of annual weeds and to conserve soil moisture during dry periods. It is highly recommended, as it makes for a labour-saving border (Fig. 4).

The most popular organic mulching materials are garden compost, well-rotted farmyard manure, peat, leafmould, spent hops, mushroom compost and shredded or pulverized bark, either chipped or partially composted bark.

The most attractive-looking of these materials are peat, leafmould, possibly mushroom compost, and certainly bark. The latter is the longest-lasting material, remaining in good condition for several years. Garden compost and farmyard manure will provide nutrients, too.

A technique you may be interested in, if you have quite a wide border, is to use a straw mulch (a cheap material) over the back half of the border where it cannot be easily seen, for it is not too attractive. Then over the front half use a more attractive-looking mulch.

Mulching material is laid evenly to a depth of 5–7.5 cm (2–3 in) in the spring. The soil should be moist, free from weeds and have received a topdressing of fertilizer. The mulch should be topped up annually if required, although some materials, like bark, will only need topping up every two or three years. To apply fertilizer to a mulched border simply sprinkle it on and then fork it into the mulch.

In some borders an inorganic mulch may be more appropriate, such as pea shingle or stone chippings. The hot dry border (see Chapter 9) could be mulched with one of these materials, for many of the plants naturally inhabit poor rocky or stony areas.

Of course, once laid, it is permanent. A layer 2.5 cm (1 in) deep of pea shingle or stone chippings will be sufficient.

PEST AND DISEASE CONTROL

Among the worst pests for many border plants are slugs and snails, which devour the soft young shoots in the spring. Plants which are particularly susceptible are hostas, lupins and delphiniums. Slug pellets

Fig. 4 An organic mulch around border plants will keep down annual weeds and conserve soil moisture during dry periods.

containing methiocarb should be sprinkled around the plants as soon as new shoots can be seen. Re-apply as necessary during the growing season, particularly around hostas, whose large mature leaves can also be rendered very unsightly by slugs and snails.

Other serious pests are aphids or greenfly which can attack many plants during spring and summer, sucking the sap and so having a weakening effect on the plants. As soon as aphids are noticed spray plants with a systemic insecticide, such as one containing the chemicals permethrin and heptenophos. This will also control many other sucking and biting insects.

Eelworm is a serious microscopic pest of border phloxes, causing deformed leaves and stems. It cannot be eradicated, so affected plants should be dug up and burnt. However, you can propagate the plants from root cuttings, as the eelworm is not found in the roots.

Among diseases, powdery mildew is the most common among border plants. Asters are particularly prone to mildew and can become completely covered with the white, powdery coating. As soon as it is noticed, spray plants with a systemic fungicide such as benomyl and repeat as necessary.

Other diseases can also be controlled with benomyl, such as iris leaf spot which shows as brown or blackish spots on the leaves. Various other plants may be affected by leaf spot, too.

STAKING

Many of the plants I recommend support themselves and therefore do not need to be provided with artificial supports. However, tall border plants with thin stems often need some help, for they can become top-heavy and are then liable to be flattened by wind and rain. Examples are the tall varieties of asters or Michaelmas daisies.

The best ways of supporting plants with this habit of growth is to insert twiggy sticks (hazel or birch) between and around the plants as they are coming into growth in the spring (Fig. 5). Make sure the height of the sticks is a bit below the flowering height of the plants. As the plants grow they will hide these supports.

Alternatively you could use proprietary metal plant supports – the type which encircle the stems to hold them in (Fig. 6). Another method is to insert several canes around each group and to encircle the stems as they grow with green garden string. Never pull in the stems too tightly, for this can spoil the natural appearance of the plants.

Some border plants, particularly delphiniums, produce several thick, heavy flower spikes and cannot therefore be supported by the above

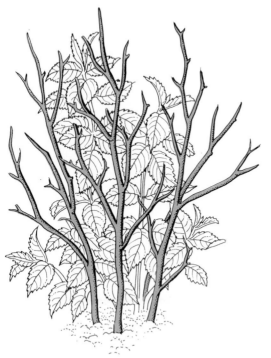

Fig. 5 Tall thin-stemmed border plants can be supported with twiggy sticks inserted soon after growth starts in spring.

Fig. 6 Proprietary metal plant supports are available in several sizes and last for years.

A mixture of compact shrubs, among them *Potentilla fruticosa*, border plants, pansies, geraniums and other summer bedding flowers sets off this house perfectly.

methods. Instead provide a stout bamboo cane for each stem before it becomes too tall, and tie it in to this as it grows with soft green garden string. If the canes are inserted behind the stems they will be inconspicuous. The canes should be slightly shorter than the ultimate height of the plants.

GENERAL TIDYING

Dead flower heads should be cut off regularly in the growing period, not only to make the plants more presentable, but also to encourage a second flush of blooms in some plants. Do not remove dead flowers, though, from any plants which are noted for attractive seed heads, like *Iris foetidissima*.

When the stems of herbaceous plants die down in the autumn they should be cut down as close as possible to the crowns of the plants. Some people do not cut them down hard enough and leave about 15 cm (6 in) of what can only be described as 'stubble'. This is of no use whatsoever to the plant and looks decidedly unsightly.

Evergreen perennials should have dead leaves removed as necessary so that they look tidy at all times.

LIFTING AND DIVIDING

Every three to four years most perennial border plants should be lifted and divided (or split into smaller portions) to keep them young and vigorous, when they will grow and flower very much better than old neglected plants.

Bear in mind, though, there are a few perennials that do not like to be disturbed and these are better left alone. Popular examples include peonies and red hot pokers. At the other extreme the asters or Michaelmas daisies are best lifted and divided every year, because they are very vigorous and so quickly deteriorate.

Some border plants cannot be divided because they do not form clumps, an example being gypsophila. Short-lived perennials like lupins and *Lychnis coronaria* are not divided, either. However, there are other methods of propagating these border plants (see pp. 29–30).

Border plants can be lifted and divided during the recommended planting times of early to mid-spring or autumn (see Chapter 3). Choose autumn only if you have a very well-drained soil.

Early spring-flowering plants are generally divided immediately after flowering, as are the spring and early summer-flowering irises.

Each clump should be lifted with a fork. Division will be easier if you

Fig. 7 Large clumps can initially be divided with two forks (*a*). The portions are further divided into hand-sized pieces for replanting (*b* and *c*).

carefully shake most of the soil away from the roots. Large clumps are best split with the aid of two garden forks (borrow one from your neighbour!). Insert these back to back through the centre of a clump and then pull the handles apart. You now have two portions, which can be split further in the same way (Fig. 7).

Divisions of a suitable size for replanting will sit comfortably in the palm of one hand. Save only the outer portions of each clump for replanting, as these are young and vigorous; discard the older, deteriorating centre.

Now for a few variations. With asters or Michaelmas daisies you can reduce clumps to single shoots with roots attached. These are replanted about 5 cm (2 in) apart each way in bold groups. Border irises which form thick fleshy rhizomes (swollen stems which grow at ground level) should be split in such a way that each division consists of a portion of rhizome (with some roots attached) and a fan of leaves (Fig. 8). When replanting iris divisions ensure the top of the rhizome remains above soil level, but the roots are well down in the soil. If necessary iris divisions can be supported with short canes until they are well rooted.

REJUVENATING THE SOIL

Of course, it is sensible to lift and divide most or all of your border plants at the same time, so that you have an empty or partially empty border, which can then be rejuvenated by digging and manuring as described in Chapter 2. Before replanting apply fertilizer and firm the soil well by treading with your heels.

While working on the border keep the roots of the plants well covered, say with damp hessian or polythene, to prevent them from drying out.

OTHER METHODS OF PROPAGATION

Division is, of course, one method of propagating or increasing border perennials, but there are other methods which can be used to bulk up your stock of plants.

Fig. 8 An iris division, consisting of a portion of rhizome with roots, and a fan of leaves.

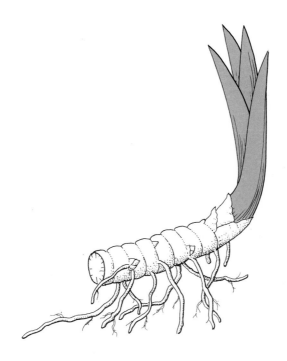

BASAL CUTTINGS

Many border perennials which produce soft young shoots from their crowns in the spring can be propagated from these. Some shoots are cut off as close as possible to the crown, when they are about 5 cm (2 in) long. They are known as basal cuttings (Fig. 9).

Insert these in pots of cutting compost, which consists of equal parts by volume of peat and sand. First, though, remove any lower leaves and dip the bases of the cuttings in homone rooting powder. Root them in a propagating case, with a basal temperature of about 18° C (65° F). When rooted pot off individually into 9 cm (3½ in) pots of John Innes potting compost No. 1. Harden off the young plants in a cold frame before planting them out in the garden.

Examples of perennials which can be propagated from basal cuttings include: *Achillea, Campanula, Chrysanthemum, Delphinium, Galega, Heliopsis, Lupinus, Lysimachia, Lythrum, Macleaya, Pyrethrum, Sidalcea* and *Thalictrum*.

Fig. 9 Basal cuttings are removed from as close to the crown of the plant as possible (*a*) and should be about 5 cm long (*b*).

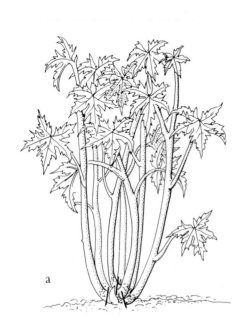

This border is planted mainly with shrubs, with a selection of flag irises at the front. Golden cornus and philadelphus bring it to life.

STEM CUTTINGS

Several border perennials can be propagated from soft side shoots in the spring and these are known as stem cuttings. Sturdy, non-flowering side shoots are removed with a sharp knife. They are prepared by cutting the base immediately below a leaf joint, to make a cutting 7.5–10 cm (3–4 in) long. Remove leaves from lower half, then dip bases in hormone rooting powder. Then the procedure is the same as for basal cuttings.

Examples of perennials which can be propagated from stem cuttings include: *Aubrieta, Centranthus, Chelone, Gentiana, Gypsophila, Linum, Nepeta, Oenothera, Penstemon, Sedum, Veronica* and *Viola*.

Other perennials are propagated from stem cuttings in the summer, once side shoots have become partially ripe or woody at the base. These are known as semi-ripe cuttings, but otherwise are prepared and rooted as above. Examples of plants increased from semi-ripe cuttings include: *Anthemis, Dianthus* and *Zauschneria*.

Fig. 10 Thick root cuttings (*a*) are inserted vertically to their entire length (*b*), while thin root cuttings (*c*) are best laid flat (*d*) and covered with a thin layer of compost.

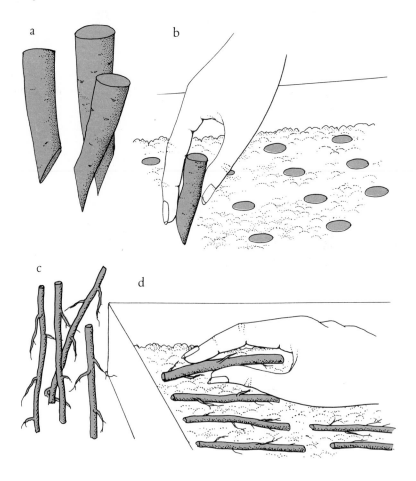

ROOT CUTTINGS

A good range of perennials can be propagated from sections of root in the autumn or early winter, especially those kinds with rather thick, fleshy roots.

When plants are dormant carefully lift and remove a few of the young thick roots. Then immediately replant the parents. The roots are then cut into 5 cm (2 in) long sections, making a flat cut at the top (always the part of the root that was nearest the crown of the plant) and a slanting cut at the bottom. This is to differentiate between tops and bottoms when inserting the cuttings (Fig. 10 a–b).

Insert cuttings vertically in trays or pots of cutting compost so that the tops are level with the surface, or slightly below it.

Phlox roots are inserted differently, because they are very thin. They are laid horizontally on the surface of compost and then covered with a 12 mm (½ in) layer of compost (Fig. 10 c–d).

Keep root cuttings in a cold frame or unheated greenhouse until late spring. If by then they have rooted and produced top growth they can be lifted and potted (as for basal cuttings). If not, leave them until the following autumn, but keep the containers in the open or in a well-ventilated cold frame over the summer.

Examples of perennials which can be propagated from root cuttings include: *Anchusa, Anemone, Crambe, Dicentra, Echinops, Eryngium, Gaillardia, Geranium, Limonium, Macleaya, Papaver, Phlox paniculata, Physalis, Primula denticulata, Stokesia, Symphytum* and *Verbascum*.

LAYERING

Dianthus (border carnations and pinks), can be increased in late summer by a method known as layering. This involves rooting shoots while they are still attached to the parent plants.

Choose young, strong, unflowered shoots and remove the leaves from the part that is to be pegged down into the soil. Then, using a sharp knife, make a cut 3.5 cm (1½ in) long halfway through a leaf joint in the stripped part of the stem (Fig. 11).

This 'tongue' should be kept open while it is being pegged down into a shallow depression in the soil. Use a piece of wire, bent to the shape of a hairpin, to hold down the shoot. The part of the shoot which is pegged should then be covered with a 5 cm (2 in) layer of soil. If your soil is heavy it would be a good idea to mix some peat and sand into the area used for layering.

Keep the soil moist and within about eight weeks the layers should have rooted, when they are cut away from the parent plant and planted elsewhere in the border.

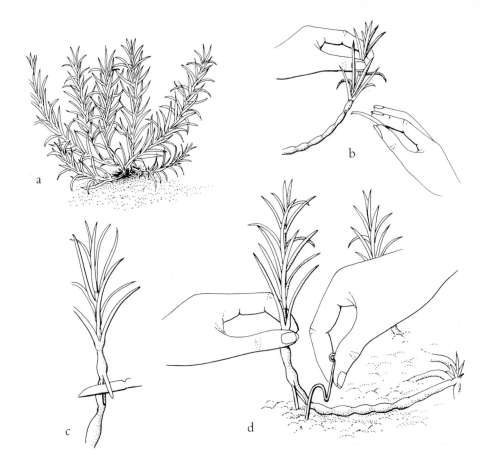

Fig. 11 Border carnations can be layered from young unflowered shoots (*a*). Remove leaves from the part to be pegged down (*b*), then cut a 'tongue' in the stripped part of the stem (*c*). Peg down with a wire peg (*d*) and cover with soil.

SEEDS

You can buy seeds of many border perennials from our leading seedsmen. Or you can save your own, but only from species, not from hybrid plants which do not come true to type.

Seeds of some perennials must be sown as soon as they are collected to ensure good germination. Well-known examples include primulas and meconopsis.

Seeds of the majority of perennials, though, are sown in late spring or early summer. Most can be sown in an outdoor seed bed, on a spare piece of ground. However, very fine or dust-like seeds, such as those of primulas, are better sown in a seed tray and germinated in a cold frame. These do not need a covering of compost.

When seeds have germinated, the seedlings from outdoor sowings should be lifted and transplanted into a nursery bed, spacing them about 30 cm (12 in) apart each way. Seedlings raised in trays are best pricked out into other trays, and then planted in a nursery bed before they become overcrowded.

By the following autumn the young plants should be large enough to plant in their flowering positions, or may be left until the following spring.

The brick path running alongside this border provides for easy mowing and maintenance. Note how its hard straight line has been masked by prostrate plants.

CHAPTER 5

MODERN BORDERS

ISLAND BEDS

Alan Bloom, of Bressingham Gardens, pioneered the method of growing hardy perennials in island beds, using plants which give a great display with the minimum of attention – in other words, no staking.

The idea is to have a group of beds with paths between them, set in a lawn, or in a paved or gravelled area, so that they can be viewed from all sides, unlike the traditional straight border backed by a hedge.

If space permits, a group of three beds looks good, but you could opt for two, or even just have a single bed if space is at a premium. It is better to have one fairly large bed rather than several very small ones which create a fussy appearance.

As indicated in Chapter 2, the beds can be formal, or regular shapes, or informal, with gently curving edges. The latter is generally preferred today and is certainly a good choice for small gardens as informality creates the illusion of more space.

CHOOSING AND GROUPING PLANTS

Plants for island beds should be self-supporting, restrained in habit (in other words, not excessively vigorous or rampant) and should be chosen to provide colour and interest for as much of the year as possible. Today, there are a great many plants which fit the bill. Rather than listing all of them indiscriminately I have decided to present you with a planting scheme containing a selection of the very best plants available – see Fig. 12.

In this scheme there are plants which flower in spring, summer and autumn. The majority bloom in the summer, the season when we need the most colour as the garden is, hopefully, being used a lot as an 'outdoor room'. The spring- and autumn-flowering plants have been well spread out over the beds, so that there is a reasonably even distribution of colour during these seasons.

I have also grouped plants pleasingly wherever possible so that we have contrast in colour and shape of flowers and foliage. Consideration has been given to heights, too. The tallest plants are set in the centre of the bed, grading down to shorter ones at the edges, although I have not been too rigid in this respect as it can create an unnatural, regimented appearance.

Do not be too worried about grouping perennials for colour contrast, though, for you will find that in nature few colours clash or look absolutely terrible together. Try to avoid, though, placing orange and pink flowers side by side, as these two colours do clash.

It is exciting combining shapes of flowers and foliage – for example, grouping plants with spikes of flowers with those which produce blooms in flat heads; or combining plants with grassy or sword-like foliage with those which have bold, rounded leaves.

Let us now take a closer look at the plants in my planting scheme. Details of their height, flowering period and number of plants required per square metre (square yard) are given in the Appendix. All of the groups in these beds are approximately 1 sq m (or 1 sq yd) in area, so each will create a bold effect.

Bed A (Fig. 12) For spring colour I have included a group of *Ranunculus gramineus*, the grass-leaved buttercup, with greyish green grassy leaves and typical deep yellow buttercup flowers. Also for spring, a doronicum or leopard's bane, with yellow daisy flowers. There are several varieties, like 'Spring Beauty' and 'Miss Mason', the former having double flowers. I have grouped doronicum with *Pulmonaria angustifolia*, a lungwort with brilliant pure blue flowers. Behind this, but flowering earlier, is *Adonis amurensis* 'Fukujukai' with yellow blooms and ferny leaves.

For late spring there is a group of *Trollius × cultorum*, with globe-shaped flowers. There are several varieties in yellow or orange, like 'Earliest of All' (yellow) and 'Fireglobe' (deep orange). Contrasting with trollius is *Ophiopogon planiscapus nigrescens*, a foliage plant with black grassy leaves. Behind these two groups is early-summer flowering *Veronica gentianoides* with spikes of light blue flowers; *V. spicata* 'Barcarole', with rose pink blooms, could be planted instead.

For autumm colour I have grouped together *Anemone hybrida*, a dwarf Michaelmas daisy or *Aster novi-belgii*, and *Sedum spectabile* with flat heads of pink flowers. There are lots of varieties of dwarf Michaelmas daisies, like 'Lady in Blue' and 'Little Pink Beauty'. Of the anemones I can recommend 'Bressingham Glow', with rose red flowers.

Another plant for autumn is *Stokesia laevis*, with large blue daisy flowers, deep blue in the variety 'Wyoming'.

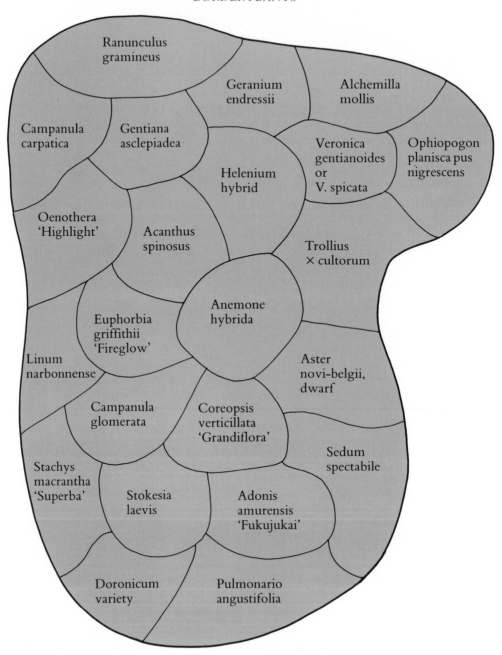

Fig. 12 These island beds (*a* and *b*) will provide colour from spring to autumn and plants have been grouped to contrast with each other.

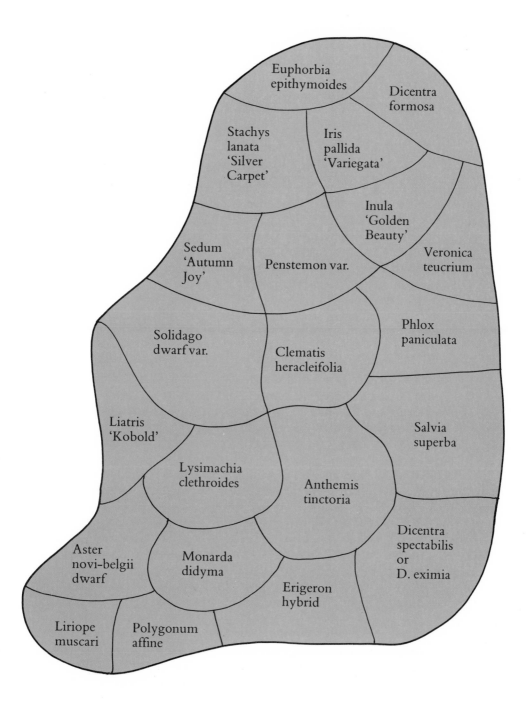

Euphorbia
epithymoides

Dicentra
formosa

Stachys
lanata
'Silver
Carpet'

Iris
pallida
'Variegata'

Inula
'Golden
Beauty'

Sedum
'Autumn
Joy'

Penstemon var.

Veronica
teucrium

Solidago
dwarf var.

Phlox
paniculata

Clematis
heracleifolia

Liatris
'Kobold'

Salvia
superba

Lysimachia
clethroides

Anthemis
tinctoria

Aster
novi-belgii
dwarf

Monarda
didyma

Dicentra
spectabilis
or
D. eximia

Erigeron
hybrid

Liriope
muscari

Polygonum
affine

A pleasing combination for early summer is *Linum narbonnense*, with bright blue flowers; the brilliant orange-red spurge, *Euphorbia griffithii* 'Fireglow'; and a bellflower, *Campanula glomerata*, an excellent variety being 'Superba' with violet flowers.

Plenty of colour in summer is provided with *Coreopsis verticillata* 'Grandiflora', which has yellow daisy flowers and ferny foliage, and *Stachys macrantha* 'Superba', with spikes of mauve-lilac flowers.

Finally a number of groups for more summer colour, including, in the centre of the bed, *Acanthus spinosus* with dramatic, deeply cut leaves and spikes of purple and white flowers. As a contrast is a daisy-flowered helenium hybrid. Good varieties are 'Coppelia', coppery orange, and 'Moerheim Beauty', bronze-red. Contrasting with this is a *Geranium endressii* variety. Choose varieties like 'A. T. Johnson', pale silvery pink, and 'Wargrave Pink', bright salmon pink. I have included, too, a group of *Gentiana asclepiadea*, a border gentian with spikes of deep blue flowers; *Oenothera* 'Highlight', with large yellow saucer-shaped flowers; and a *Campanula carpatica* variety, a good one being 'Isobel' with deep blue bells. A bold group of lime green *Alchemilla mollis*, or lady's mantle, contrasts well with the geranium and ophiopogon.

Bed B (Fig. 12) At the top of this bed is a pleasant spring combination of the dwarf lime green spurge, *Euphorbia epithymoides*, and *Dicentra formosa*, a good variety being 'Bountiful' with purplish crimson blooms and ferny foliage. Foliage plants which contrast well with these two are *Iris pallida* 'Variegata', with sword-like leaves striped cream and greyish green, and *Stachys lanata* 'Silver Carpet' with silvery woolly foliage.

Spring colour at the bottom of this bed can be provided with more dicentras, such as *D. spectabilis*, bleeding heart, with red heart-shaped flowers and ferny foliage, or *D. eximia*, also with attractive foliage but with pink flowers.

Down the left-hand side of the bed we have plenty of autumn colour from plants like *Sedum* 'Autumn Joy' with flat heads of salmon pink flowers. Contrasting with this is a dwarf golden rod or solidago with yellow flowers. Good varieties are 'Cloth of Gold' and 'Golden Thumb'. *Liatris* 'Kobold', with its spikes of deep lilac flowers, should still be in flower (a good contrast), and in the centre of the bed is a group of *Lysimachia clethroides* with curved spikes of off-white flowers.

At the edge of the bed another dwarf Michaelmas daisy or *Aster novi-belgii* (see earlier mention), and to contrast with this a group of *Liriope muscari,* with grassy leaves and spikes of violet-mauve flowers. Effective with a *Polygonum affine* variety, with a spreading habit and small spikes of pink or red flowers. Good varieties are 'Darjeeling Red' and 'Donald Lowndes', both deep pink. It will still be flowering in autumn.

For summer colour in this bed I have included *Inula* 'Golden Beauty' with deep yellow daisy flowers. I cannot resist veronicas, so have included *Veronica teucrium*. There are several excellent varieties, like 'Crater Lake Blue' (deep blue), 'Kapitan' (bright blue), 'Shirley Blue' (bright blue) and 'Trehane' (deep blue).

Penstemon hybrids make an excellent show in summer and should be included in every island bed. They have somewhat tubular flowers, and good varieties include 'Catherine de la Mare', lilac-blue flowers; 'Cherry Ripe', rich red; 'Firebird', scarlet; 'Garnet', deep red; 'King George', salmon red; and 'Ruby', red. Give penstemons a little protection in winter, by covering the crowns with dry bracken or straw, as a severe winter can kill some varieties.

In the centre of the bed I have included a herbaceous clematis, *C. heracleifolia*, which poduces masses of small, fragrant, blue flowers. There is a form called *davidiana* which has flowers in a deeper shade of blue. Contrasting well with this is a group of *Anthemis tinctoria* with yellow daisy flowers. There are several varieties of this including 'Mrs Buxton' and 'Wargrave', both of which have pale yellow blooms. Contrasting very well with the anthemis is a herbaceous sage, *Salvia superba*, which carries its violet-purple flower in spikes. Varieties I can recommend include 'East Friesland', 'Lubeca', 'May Night', and, in a different colour, 'Rose Queen', with rose pink blooms.

Every island bed should have some groups of the border phlox, *P. paniculata*. Choose the lower-growing varieties for beds, like 'Bill Green', pink with a crimson centre; 'Chintz' and 'Eva Cullum', both pink with a red centre; 'Franz Schubert', lilac; 'Fujiyama', white; 'Hampton Court', blue; 'Mary Fox', salmon with a red centre; 'Mother of Pearl', white, flushed pink; 'Sandringham', shocking pink; and 'White Admiral', pure white.

Varieties of *Monarda didyma* are an excellent choice for summer flowering in an island bed. Popularly known as oswego tea, the flowers are carried in whorled heads. The varieties come in various colours: there is 'Blue Stocking' with violet-purple blooms; 'Cambridge Scarlet', a great favourite in red; the equally popular 'Croftway Pink', with clearest pink blooms; 'Prairie Night' in deepest violet-purple; and 'Snow Maiden', white.

And last, but not least, I have included a group of erigeron or fleabane. The erigerons are 'made' for island beds and there are lots of varieties to choose from. They have daisy-like blooms. Choose from

This border gains in interest from the curve of the lawn which draws one forward to see what is growing around the bend.

'Adria', lavender blue; 'Amity', lilac pink; 'Charity', pale pink; 'Darkest of All', dark violet blue; 'Dignity', violet blue; 'Foerster's Liebling', deep pink; 'Prosperity', pale blue; and 'Schwarzes Meer', dark lavender violet.

THE MIXED BORDER

For many people this may be a more attractive proposition than island beds of perennials, for in a mixed border many more kinds of plants are grown. It is safe to say that a great proportion of small gardens have mixed borders of some kind.

A mixed border can again be formal or informal, as discussed in Chapter 2. It will need a background of some kind and ideas for this will again be found in Chapter 2.

This border has a permanent framework of shrubs, both flowering and foliage kinds, deciduous and evergreen. A good balance in any border is one-third evergreen shrubs and two-thirds deciduous, to avoid a very heavy or sombre effect.

Among the shrubs are planted other subjects of your choice, such as spring-flowering bulbs; summer-flowering bulbs including lilies; roses

The boldly contrasting colours of a golden cut-leaved elder, a purple-leaved berberis and blue-flowered delphiniums put drama into this planting.

(especially shrub roses, rather than the more formal large-flowered and cluster-flowered bush roses); and hardy annuals.

Hardy perennials play a very important part in mixed borders but not all kinds are suitable by any means. It is a case of choosing those which associate well with shrubs. This rules out many of the really flamboyant or garish flowers. Perennials that go well with shrubs are those with a more natural-looking habit of growth. Indeed, many of the plants I will recommend are species or wild plants, as opposed to man-made hybrids, although I have included some of the latter.

In the mixed border we should aim for interest and colour over all four seasons, and I have taken this into account in my choice of suitable perennials. Also, we should be conscious of grouping plants to good effect, aiming for contrasts in flower and leaf colour, flower and leaf shape, and even texture of foliage.

The perennials should be planted in bold groups and drifts among the shrubs. I like to combine plants from the seasonal point of view: in other words, grouping spring-flowering perennials with spring-flowering shrubs; autumn-flowering kinds with shrubs noted for autumn leaf colour and berries, and so on.

Some of the perennials I have chosen are low-growing or prostrate kinds, making excellent ground cover between shrubs. The use of ground cover plants makes for maintenance-free areas, as you do not have to carry out weeding or soil cultivations once the plants have established and formed a dense carpet of growth.

CHOOSING AND GROUPING PLANTS

Details of height, flowering period and number of plants required per square metre (square yard) are given in the Appendix. I suggest, for best effect, groups no smaller than 1 sq m (1 sq yd) in area.

I am very fond of acanthus or bear's breeches, as it is trouble-free and creates a very dramatic effect wherever used. For the mixed border I can recommend the species *Acanthus longifolius*, which has long, deeply cut, wavy, dark green leaves. The plant is worth growing for these alone, but in the summer it sends up tall spikes of lilac-coloured flowers. This acanthus associates well with many shrubs, but I particularly like to group it with pink shrub roses, which flower at the same time, and with the deciduous foliage shrub, *Cotinus coggygria*

Fig. 13 A beautiful combination for summer colour in the mixed border: *Acanthus longifolius, Cotinus coggygria* 'Foliis Purpureis' and a pink shrub rose.

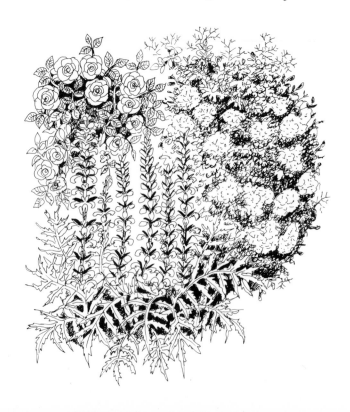

'Foliis Purpureis', which has deep plum purple leaves (Fig. 13). The variety 'Royal Purple' has dark wine purple foliage. This is a stunning combination for summer colour in the mixed border.

Agapanthus or African lilies (they are not true lilies) are natural companions for shrubs. They have long strap-shaped leaves and, in late summer and early autumn, roundish heads of tubular flowers. Try *Agapanthus campanulatus* 'Isis', with deep blue flowers. It is one of the hardiest types (some are decidedly tender). Also highly recommended are the Headbourne hybrids which come in various shades of blue. These also rank among the hardiest of the African lilies.

I like to create an autumn scene with agapanthus and complementary shrubs. Shrubs with good leaf colour include *Cotinus coggygria* 'Flame', whose leaves turn brilliant orange; and *Parrotia persica*, which turns gold and crimson. Shrubs with bright autumn berries include the many cotoneasters and a wide range of berberis or barberries, like the hybrids 'Bountiful' and 'Pirate King'. The spindle, *Euonymus europaeus* 'Red Cascade', has colourful autumn fruits and foliage.

Another autumn spectacle, perhaps in a different part of the border, can be created with pampas grass, or *Cortaderia selloana* varieties. This grass forms great clumps of arching foliage and majestic plumes of flowers. The species can be grown if desired and it has white plumes. 'Sunningdale Silver' is a well-known variety, with creamy white plumes. You might like to try a comparatively new variety called 'Gold Band'. This has golden yellow and green foliage and silver plumes of flowers. It is grown as much for its foliage as for its flowers.

I also like to back clumps of pampas grass with shrubs which have good autumn colour and berries. I have mentioned several above, but you may also like to include some Japanese maples, varieties of *Acer palmatum* like 'Heptalobum Elegans' or 'Heptalobum Osakazuki', with brilliant autumn foliage.

You may think it a bit odd to grow vegetables in the mixed border, but two perennial kinds, the cardoon, *Cynara cardunculus*, and the globe artichoke, *Cynara scolymus*, have the most beautiful foliage and are worth growing purely as decorative plants. The cardoon has deeply cut, silver-grey leaves which can attain a length of at least 1 m (3 ft). Grey stems appear in summer, carrying large thistle-like flowers, purple in colour. The globe artichoke also has large, dramatic foliage, but it is not so grey as that of the cardoon. This also has large thistle-like blooms in summer, this time blue. You will no doubt wish to harvest the flower buds before they open, for they are a great delicacy, but this will not detract from the beauty of the plant.

So which shrubs make suitable companions for cardoons and globe artichokes? I suggest purple-leaved shrubs as a background. I have already mentioned purple cotinus; another good one is a purple-leaved berberis, *B. × ottawensis* 'Purpurea' (also known as 'Superba'). This has large oval leaves, very deep purple in colour. You could then complete the group with some pink-flowered shrub roses, which look lovely with the grey foliage of the cynaras. 'Ballerina' is a marvellous apple-blossom pink with a white centre to each flower. The single flowers are small, but born in profusion.

Two ornamental grasses I would not be without are *Helictotrichon sempervirens* and *Festuca glauca*. The first makes dense clumps of narrow, blue-grey leaves. The festuca, or fescue, is a dwarf clump-forming species, also with thin leaves, this time grey-blue. Grow these in bold groups or drifts when they form good ground cover. They go well with many shrubs and make a particularly attractive underplanting for red or pink shrub roses.

There are some perennials which I like to associate with golden-foliage shrubs, such as the ever-popular golden mock orange, *Philadelphus coronarius* 'Aureus', the golden-variegated *Elaeagnus pungens* 'Maculata' and the yellow-leaved *Berberis thunbergii* 'Aurea'. These shrubs make a lovely backdrop for eryngiums, like *Eryngium alpinum* with deeply cut leaves and thistle-like flower heads in a vivid metallic blue; and *E. tripartitum* which has deep green leaves and globe-shaped flower heads in greyish blue. Then there are the globe thistles, such as *Echinops ritro* with attractive greyish green foliage and steel blue globe-shaped flowers.

A distinctive spurge for the mixed border is *Euphorbia sikkimensis* with greenish yellow flower heads in the summer. Front this with a grey-leaved shrub, such as *Senecio* 'Sunshine' (also known as *S. greyi*). It produces yellow daisy flowers which I prefer to cut off before they open.

Some ground-cover plants for associating with shrubs and roses include *Geranium sanguineum*, a crane's-bill with magenta-purple flowers, and its varieties 'Album', white, and *lancastriense* 'Splendens' with rose pink blooms. Also good ground cover is *Prunella grandiflora* (also known as *P. webbiana*), forming mats of foliage. Usual varieties include 'Loveliness', lilac; 'Pink Loveliness' and 'White Loveliness'.

Stachys lanata 'Silver Carpet' is the non-flowering form of lamb's ears and is a marvellous carpeting plant, with its felted silvery leaves which last all year round, although in a wet winter they can look a bit tatty. But plenty of new growth is put out in spring. Indeed, this is a vigorous grower, but never becomes troublesome as it is easily forked out if it outgrows its allotted space. I like to lift and divide stachys at least every two years, using single rooted shoots for replanting. Stachys

Richly varied leaf shapes from the bold bergenias at the front to the thistle-leaved echinops contribute as much to this planting as the flowers.

makes a superb underplanting for pink or red shrub roses.

The Lenten rose, *Helleborus orientalis*, flowers in winter and spring and is a marvellous subject for mass-planting around winter- and spring-flowering shrubs, such as the witch hazel, *Hamamelis mollis* 'Pallida', with yellow blooms; the yellow-flowered Cornelian cherry, *Cornus mas*; the forsythias; and the winter-flowering heathers, varieties of *Erica herbacea*. Include in this scheme some shrubs noted for their coloured bark, like the shrubby dogwood, *Cornus alba* 'Sibirica', with red stems, and *C. stolonifera* 'Flaviramea' with yellow bark.

The evergreen Lenten rose carries bowl-shaped flowers and colours include white, cream, pink, red, purple and crimson. Often the flowers are spotted on the inside. The plants found in garden centres are generally hybrids. Particularly worth trying to obtain are the Raithby hybrids, which are all named and include some unusual colours and spectacular spotting.

Hemerocallis hybrids, or day lilies, really are excellent perennials in every way. They are easy to grow and have an incredibly long flowering period. They form bold clumps of grassy foliage and have lily-like flowers in a wide range of colours, each flower lasting for only one day.

Day lilies look lovely planted among rhododendrons and azaleas but associate very well with many other shrubs.

Some excellent varieties include 'Black Magic', deep reddish mahogany; 'Bonanza', light orange; 'Doubloon', golden yellow; 'Fandango', deep orange; 'George Cunningham', pink; 'Giant Moon', pale yellow; 'Golden Chimes', golden yellow; 'Hyperion', pure yellow; 'Neyron Rose', rose red; 'Pink Damask', pink; 'Stafford', deep red; 'Stella d'Oro', canary yellow, dwarf; 'Varsity', pale peach; and 'Zora', a dwarf orange.

New American day lilies worth looking out for include 'Anzac', brilliant red, very large flowers; 'Canary Glow', vivid canary yellow; 'Cherry Cheeks', huge cherry red flowers; and 'Luxury Lace', small ruffled flowers in creamy lavender pink with lime green throat.

Kniphofias or red hot pokers look lovely with shrubs noted for autumn leaf colour and berries, as they are in flower during that season. My favourite red hot poker is *Kniphofia caulescens* with greyish foliage (the leaves of kniphofias are grassy), and spikes of light red flowers. There are many named hybrids available, too, like 'Ada', deep orange flowers; 'Fiery Fred', brilliant orange; 'Firefly', orange-red; 'Bressingham Hybrids' in mixed colours; 'Candlelight', clear yellow; 'Little Maid', dwarf, ivory flowers; and 'Percy's Pride', cream, tinged green and yellow.

Macleaya cordata, the plume poppy, goes well with many shrubs but place it towards the back of the border as it's a tall plant. It has lobed greyish leaves and panicles of creamy white blooms. However, try not to hide the plume poppy with other subjects for the whole plant is attractive.

Two grasses which are 'made' for the mixed border are the zebra grass, *Miscanthus sinensis* 'Zebrinus', with gold-banded leaves; and the very vigorous gardener's garters, *Phalaris arundinacea* 'Picta', with green and white striped leaves. I think these grasses look good with large-leaved shrubs, such as *Fatsia japonica* and the mahonias. Gardener's garters look superb, too, with purple-leaved shrubs – I have recommended several of these above. You will have to keep on top of it, though, for it will soon exceed its allotted space, spreading vigorously by underground rhizomes. However, it is easy enough to dig up with a fork. I generally lift, divide and replant it every couple of years.

Phormiums, or New Zealand flax, have become very popular in recent years due to the introduction of dwarf kinds with colourful foliage – some look almost like tropical plants. Phormiums have evergreen sword-shaped leaves and therefore make good companions for shrubs with rounded foliage. Drainage must be excellent or they may succumb to root rot over the winter, and it's fair to say that they can suffer, or even be killed, in a hard winter.

Of the dwarf *Phormium tenax* varieties I can recommend 'Maori Sunrise', which has pinkish leaves banded with orange and edged with bronze, this being one of the most colourful varieties; 'Sundowner' with grey-purple leaves edged creamy pink; and 'Yellow Wave' with yellow leaves edged with green. *Phormium tenax* 'Purpureum' is a tall plant with purplish leaves.

Dwarf *Phormium cookianum* varieties worth growing are 'Cream Delight' with cream leaves edged with green; and 'Tricolor' which is striped bright green and white and edged with red.

What an amazing variety of unusual plants, including dwarf roses and dark-leaved cannas, is set together in this moist border in Beth Chatto's Essex garden.

CHAPTER 6

THE TRADITIONAL HERBACEOUS BORDER

Borders containing only hardy perennials, backed by a hedge, and with a lawn or grass path in front, were popular features of private gardens earlier in this century, but then they went out of favour.

The herbaceous border is the very essence of an English garden, though, and with the resurgent interest in the English style of gardening (which includes cottage gardens: see Chapter 7), I feel it is appropriate at this time to put a strong case for the herbaceous border.

The reason the herbaceous border went out of favour was that it was labour-intensive, because it contained a lot of very tall perennials which needed supporting; and many of the older varieties of herbaceous plants were very rampant and needed to be kept under control by frequent lifting and division – a prime example being the golden rod or solidago.

However, today we have a very wide selection of perennials which do not need staking, and many of these could be used in a herbaceous border. Also, there are available more restrained varieties of hitherto rampant plants – again I quote as an example the golden rod or solidago. By choosing such varieties you automatically reduce time involved in border maintenance.

So, how does a herbaceous border differ from an island bed as far as plants are concerned? We certainly use more taller plants, obviously at the back of the border, and to be honest some of these will have to be provided with supports, so this does make the border a little more labour-intensive than an island bed. But the keen gardener will surely not object to this, for after all he or she will want to be gardening rather than sitting and looking. The herbaceous border gives us the ideal place for growing the stately delphiniums, verbascums and other towering plants.

In the centre and at the front of the border we obviously have shorter plants, and most of these can be the self-supporting kinds.

The traditional concept of a herbaceous border is to provide abundant colour in the summer, and I think we should stick to this. The English garden is largely a summer garden: that is when it us used the most. In my planting plan for a traditional herbaceous border, Fig. 14, you will therefore find many perennials which flower in the summer. However, I have also included quite a few, too, which flower very early on (some in the spring), and certainly a good selection for autumn. So colour and interest spans three seasons. Sadly, such a border has no interest whatsoever in the winter.

If, therefore, you feel your garden is not large enough to take a border which has no winter interest, then I would advise you to opt for the mixed border. Certainly you do need a reasonably large garden to take a herbaceous border, so that there is room, too, for other beds and borders which can provide colour and interest at other times of year, including winter.

Having discussed the pros and cons of the herbaceous border, and obviously very much in favour of this method of growing perennials, you may be wondering if I have one in my garden. I do indeed have a true herbaceous border, and I can say that it is not very much more time-consuming to maintain than an island bed. I have to do a certain amount of staking, and this probably takes me about half a day each year – the supports are all put in as the plants are starting into growth in the spring.

I mulch the border to cut down on weeding. At the end of the season all the dead stems have to be cut down – but this also applies to island beds. Plants are lifted and divided every three or four years.

I derive a great deal of pleasure from this border, which provides a bank of virtually solid colour, at least 1.8 m (6 ft) high at the back.

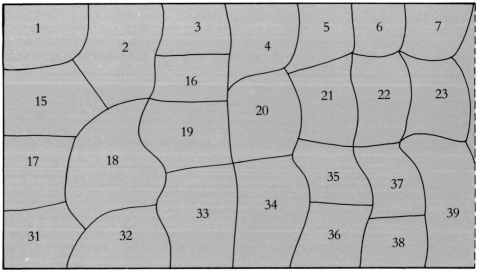

Each group appx 1m² (1 sq yd)

CHOOSING AND GROUPING PLANTS

As with the island beds, I am presenting a planting scheme, Fig. 14, which contains a range of excellent border plants to provide colour in spring, summer and autumn. Heights, numbers of plants required per sq m (sq yd) and flowering periods are given in the Appendix. Each group in my planting plan is approximately 1 sq m (or 1 sq yd) in area, to ensure a bold effect.

Fig. 14 A traditional herbaceous border, to provide colour from spring to autumn. 1, *Campanula latifolia*. 2, *Artemisia lactiflora*. 3, *Helianthus multiflorus* variety. 4, *Delphinium* hybrid. 5, *Achillea filipendulina* 'Gold Plate'. 6, *Eupatorium purpureum* 'Atropurureum'. 7, *Solidago*, tall variety. 8, *Artemisia ludoviciana*. 9, *Aster novae-angliae* variety. 10, *Eremurus* hybrid. 11, *Campanula lactiflora*. 12, *Verbascum* hybrid. 13, *Heliopsis patula*. 14, *Crambe cordifolia*. 15, *Echinacea purpurea*. 16, *Lysimachia punctata*. 17, *Paeonia lactiflora*. 18, *Gaillardia* variety. 19, *Lupinus* hybrid. 20, *Iris germanica* variety. 21, *Lythrum virgatum* 'The Rocket'. 22, *Aster novi-belgii* variety. 23, *Physalis franchetii*. 24, *Polygonum bistorta* 'Superbum'. 25, *Chrysanthemum maximum*. 26, *Thalictrum dipterocarpum* 'Hewitt's Double'. 27, *Helenium* hybrid. 28, *Gypsophila paniculata*. 29, *Phlox paniculata* variety. 30, *Aster acris*. 31, *Tradescantia virginiana*. 32, *Geum* × *borisii*. 33, *Anaphalis triplinervis* 'Summer Snow'. 34, *Lychnis viscaria* 'Splendens Plena'. 35, *Pyrethrum* variety. 36, *Limonium latifolium* 'Violetta'. 37, *Chelone barbata*. 38, *Liatris spicata*. 39, *Rudbeckia fulgida* 'Goldsturm'. 40, *Geum chiloense* variety. 41, *Dictamnus fraxinella*. 42, *Papaver orientale*. 43, *Centaurea dealbata*. 44, *Scabiosa caucasica*. 45, *Physostegia virginiana*. 46, *Heuchera* variety. 47, *Crocosmia* hybrid.

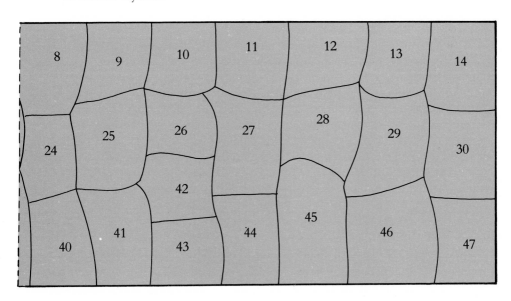

Plants which flower early in the season and in the autumn have been well distributed over the border, and the summer-flowering subjects planted among them. I have tried to group plants effectively, too, taking into account flower colours and shapes. The tallest plants are at the back, grading down to the front with shorter plants, although there are some taller and shorter plants 'drifting' towards the centre of the border.

Early colour Plants which flower early in the season, in spring or early summer, include lupin (*Lupinus*) hybrids with bold spikes of flowers. Still the best in my opinion are the 'Russell Hybrids' in a good mixture of colours. I also like 'Chandelier', in shades of yellow; 'The Chatelaine', pink and white; 'The Governor', blue and white; and 'The Pages' in shades of carmine.

Good companions for lupins are varieties of *Iris germanica*, or tall bearded irises. These come in many colours, such as 'Amethyst Flame', violet and purple; 'Berkeley Gold', deep yellow; 'Dancer's Veil', white and violet; 'Frost and Flame', white, with orange 'beard'; 'Jane Phillips', light blue; and 'Sable', dark violet-purple.

Paeonia lactiflora varieties are essential herbaceous-border plants with their huge double flowers. They are best not lifted and divided once planted for they do not like root disturbance. They are very long-lived perennials and will remain in good condition for a great many years. Popular varieties are 'Bowl of Beauty', deep pink with cream centre; 'Duchesse de Nemours', white; 'President Poincaré', carmine; 'President Roosevelt', deep red; and 'Sarah Bernhardt', pale pink.

Large flamboyant blooms are produced by varieties of the Oriental poppy, *Papaver orientale*. I can recommend 'Harvest Moon', deep orange; 'Ladybird', vermilion red; 'Mrs Perry', salmon pink; 'Perry's White', white; and 'Turkish Delight', palest pink.

Pyrethrums are rather floppy plants and are best provided with twiggy sticks for support. They produce daisy-like flowers and good varieties include 'Brenda', deep pink; 'Bressingham Red', red; and 'Princess Mary', double flowers in palest pink.

A massive perennial for the back of the border is *Crambe cordifolia* which blooms in late spring. You must make space for its large leaves, above which tower huge panicles of white flowers.

Geums flower in early summer and make bright splashes of colour at the front of the border. Very popular is G. × *borisii* with large orange blooms. Varieties of G. *chiloense* are also well worth border space, like double yellow 'Lady Stratheden' and double brilliant orange-red 'Mrs Bradshaw'.

Another corner of Beth Chatto's garden, dependent more on the shapes of the plants – bold-leaved hostas and tall spiky veratrums – than on flower colour.

Heucheras start flowering in late spring and have dainty sprays of small flowers. Good modern varieties include 'Firebird', deep red; 'Hyperion', deep pink; and 'Bressingham Hybrids' in mixed colours.

I have used in my plan *Lychnis viscaria* 'Splendens Plena' to hide the iris partially after it has flowered. It flowers from early to mid-summer and has cerise-coloured double blooms.

Late colour These, then, are my recommendations for early colour in the border. But what about colour later in the year – in late summer and autumn?

The main subjects for autumn colour are the tall varieties of asters or Michaelmas daisies, like *Aster acris* with huge heads of lavender blue flowers. It needs supporting well or it will be laid flat by wind and rain. Contrasting well with this at the front of the border is a group of crocosmia. Hybrids are grown, like 'Emily MacKenzie' with deep orange flowers; 'Vulcan', deep orange-red; and *C. masonorum* 'Firebird', rich reddish orange.

At the back of the border I have included a group of *Aster novae-angliae*. Good varieties are 'Alma Potschke', rose and salmon flowers; 'Harrington's Pink', very well-known, a rich shade of pink; and 'September Ruby', brillant ruby red blooms. In the centre of the border I have included a group of *Aster novi-belgii*. Choose a tall variety, like 'Freda Ballard' with deep red semi-double flowers; 'Marie Ballard', light blue double flowers; and 'Winston S. Churchill', a highly popular variety with brilliant ruby red blooms. These tall asters need the support of twiggy sticks as they can be flattened by rain and wind.

Next to the *Aster novi-belgii* I have placed a goup of *Physalis franchetii* which bears orange-red 'lanterns' in the autumn (these are seed capsules and they last for many weeks.)

At the back of the border are two artemisias which bloom in late summer and autumn: *A. lactiflora* with big plumes of cream flowers and *A. ludoviciana* which has white woolly foliage and panicles of silvery white flowers. Both have aromatic leaves.

Chelone barbata flowers in summer but continues into autumn. It carries spikes of tubular flowers, rose red in colour. *Chrysanthemum maximum* varieties also continue into autumn and are valued for their white daisy flowers, which contrast well with spiky blooms. An old very well-known variety is 'Esther Read' with double blooms. Also double is 'Wirral Supreme'.

Echinacea purpurea varieties are excellent border plants with their large daisy flowers in summer and through to early autumn. The species itself is also worth growing and has crimson-purple blooms. Variety 'Robert Bloom' has reddish purple flowers. In my plan the echinacea has a superb background of *Artemisia lactiflora*, and it goes well, too, with the *Campanula latifolia*.

For the back of the border I can recommend *Eupatorium purpureum* 'Atropurpureum' which blooms in late summer/autumn, carrying rose-lilac blooms above attractive purplish foliage. It makes a nice companion for the tall golden rod or solidago. There are several good varieties of solidago including 'Mimosa' with sprays of yellow flowers.

No border should be without a group of heleniums with their daisy-like flowers. There are plenty of good varieties and I can particularly recommend 'Bruno', reddish mahogany; 'Butterpat', yellow; and the all-time favourite, 'Moerheim Beauty', bronze-red. I also like 'Copper Spray' with coppery red flowers.

Helianthus multiflorus varieties flower into the autumn. This is the perennial sunflower with deep yellow blooms in varieties 'Loddon Gold' and 'Morning Sun'. In my plan this group contrasts well with artemisias and delphiniums.

Lythrums carry their flowers in spikes from mid-summer through to autumn. I have used the popular *L. virgatum* 'The Rocket' with rose red flowers, but equally good are the *L. salicaria* varieties like 'Firecandle', rose red; 'Robert', pink; and 'The Beacon', deep rose red.

The border phloxes, varieties of *Phlox paniculata*, start flowering in mid-summer and carry on into autumn. My group contrasts nicely with gypsophila. There are lots of varieties to choose from and among the taller ones I can recommend 'Border Gem', violet-purple; 'Cherry Pink', carmine pink; 'Excelsior', deep lilac pink; 'Prince of Orange', brilliant orange salmon; 'Red Indian', brilliant crimson; and 'Starfire', deep red.

Flowering in summer and into autumn is *Physostegia virginiana*. There are several varieties but a low-growing one for the front of the border is 'Vivid' with short spikes of deep rose flowers. Also with a long flowering season, well into autumn, are the rudbeckias with their daisy flowers, which should be in every border. I have chosen *R. fulgida* 'Goldsturm' which has golden flowers with a black centre. Also very desirable is *R. deamii*, popularly known as black-eyed Susan. This, too, is yellow with a black centre to the flowers.

Also continuing their summer display into autumn are the varieties of *Scabiosa caucasica*, or scabious, which in this border contrast well with physostegia. Popular varieties are 'Clive Greaves' with typical blue flowers, and the white 'Miss Wilmott'.

More colour for summer Let us now consider further perennials for summer colour. Among my great favourites are the achilleas with their flat heads of yellow flowers which contrast so beautifully in shape and colour with the stately spikes of delphiniums. *Achillea filipendulina* 'Gold Plate' is the one in the planting scheme and it has bright yellow flowers. 'Moonshine' is another excellent variety, with light yellow blooms and grey foliage. It is much shorter so needs to be placed towards the front of a border. Although not in my planting scheme I

Moisture-loving pink astilbes, lilac-flowered hostas with bold ribbed leaves and yellow lilies provide the interest in this thickly planted border.

must mention *A. ptarmica* 'The Pearl', a 'middle-of-the-border' plant with double, button-like white blooms.

Anaphalis triplinervis 'Summer Snow' is used in this border to hide the foliage of the lupins once they have finished flowering (when they are least attractive). The anaphalis has greyish foliage and white flowers and is a useful plant for separating strongly coloured plants.

The bellflowers or campanulas are classed among the 'essential' border plants with their spikes of bell-shaped blooms. I have used *Campanula latifolia*, good varieties being 'Gloaming', light blue and *macrantha*, violet-purple; and *C. lactiflora* with lavender blue flowers. A good variety of this is 'Loddon Anna', palest pink. Although not in this planting scheme, the peach-leaved bellflower is also well worth growing. Botanically *C. persicifolia*, it has some good varieties like 'Telham Beauty' with large blue flowers, and 'Hampstead White', pure white.

In this border *Centaurea dealbata* effectively hides the 'tatty' foliage of the Oriental poppy when that has finished its display. The daisy-like flowers are pink in the variety 'John Coutts' and very deep pink in 'Steenbergii', which has silver-grey leaves.

Delphiniums with their stately fat spikes of blooms contrast well in shape and colour with helianthus and achillea. Popular are the 'Pacific Hybrids' in shades of blue, white and pink, but new on the market are the 'New Century' hybrid delphiniums in similar colours. It is said these are longer-lived than the 'Pacific Hybrids' and have even stronger spikes of flowers.

Dictamnus fraxinella (also known as *D. albus*) is the burning bush which is strongly aromatic and bears spikes of scented white flowers. There is also a pink-flowered form.

The eremurus hybrids, or foxtail lilies, are truly majestic border plants with their substantial towering spikes of flowers. The best varieties have the prefix 'Highdown'. There is 'Highdown Pink', pale pink; 'Highdown Yellow', a good shade of yellow; and 'Highdown White'.

Gaillardias are very showy, almost gaudy perennials but are considered among the 'essential' border plants. They have large daisy-like flowers, bright yellow in 'Croftway Yellow', deep yellow with a red centre in 'Goblin', and orange-red in 'Mandarin'.

Gypsophila paniculata is so useful for contrasting with brightly coloured border plants and for separating colours which might otherwise clash. It has 'clouds' of tiny white flowers. The variety 'Bristol Fairy' is the one usually grown, but for a change I can recommend the double pink 'Flamingo'.

Heliopsis patula contrasts here with the spires of verbascum. It has large bright yellow daisy flowers and is quite a vigorous grower but not sufficiently so to be considered a troublesome perennial.

Liatris spicata produces spikes of flowers which open from the top downwards. The blooms are purplish and provide a show over many months. A highly recommended front-of-the-border perennial. Here it contrasts well with *Limonium latifolium* 'Violetta', a sea lavender with sprays of violet flowers.

Although not in my planting scheme, I cannot write about summer-flowering border plants without including a few more lychnis or campions. Very popular, on account of its brilliant scarlet flowers, is *L. chalcedonica*. The blooms are in the shape of a Maltese cross. The *L. coronaria* varieties are also very good border plants, although short-lived, and have silvery grey leaves and stems. The flowers, very freely produced over a long season, are rose pink in the variety 'Abbotswood Rose' and red in 'Atrosanguinea'.

The yellow loosestrife, *Lysimachia punctata*, is a vigorous spreader and has to be kept under control, but is very appealing with its spikes of cup-shaped bright yellow flowers which bloom over a long period.

The pink spikes of *Polygonum bistorta* 'Superbum', one of the knotweeds, contrast nicely with the white daisy flowers of *Chrysanthemum maximum*. This is an invasive knotweed, especially in moist fertile soil, but well worth growing for its long succession of flowers.

Thalictrum dipterocarpum 'Hewitt's Double' is a meadow rue with sprays of double mauve flowers and it does best in good fertile soil. *Tradescantia virginiana* varieties never seem to be out of flower in the summer and are well worth growing on this account, although their grassy foliage is not particularly tidy. The three-petalled flowers are mainly in shades of blue or purple, as well as white. Good varieties are 'Isis', deep blue; 'Osprey', white; 'Pauline', lilac; 'Purple Dome', purple; and 'Zwanenburg Blue', large pure blue flowers. An unusual colour is found in the variety 'Carmine Glow'.

The traditional herbaceous border is the place for the verbascum hybrids, or mulleins, which produce their flowers in tall, stately spires. Here they contrast with the daisy flowers of heliopsis and the bells of *Campanula lactiflora*. Probably the best known is 'Gainsborough', with pale yellow blooms and attractive grey leaves. Also with grey foliage is the white-flowered 'Mont Blanc'. 'Cotswold Queen' has biscuit-yellow flowers. Not so tall as these is 'Pink Domino', suitable for the centre of a border and carrying deep pink blooms.

So that is my selection for a traditional herbaceous border. I have them all in my own border and feel sure you will enjoy growing them.

CHAPTER 7

THE COTTAGE GARDEN BORDER

What is a cottage garden? It is an English style of gardening and many of the early ones (of the sixteenth and seventeenth centuries) which belonged to better-off members of society, were laid out very formally, with geometric beds and paths between them. They were probably planted mainly with medicinal plants and herbs, with perhaps a few ornamental plants here and there. Not exactly most people's idea of a cottage garden.

Furthermore, it seems unlikely that the tiny gardens of those cottagers who spent a hard life working on the land were a mass of colourful, well-tended plants, as many people today believe. It is more likely that all the ground available was put to more practical use – for growing food crops to supplement meagre wages.

But when working conditions improved in this century, and people had more time and money to indulge in decorative plants, many cottage gardens certainly became a glorious mixture of colourful plants, generally without an overall planting or colour scheme. Vegetables were often grown among the flowers, which included perennials as well as annuals, bulbs, shrubs and climbers – like roses and honeysuckle around the door. The odd apple tree grew here and there to provide shade as well as fruit. This is certainly our idea of a cottage garden today, but although such a garden appears just to have happened, this cannot be the case, for intensive planting of this kind has to be kept under control: plants have to be lifted, divided and replanted, or cut back, as they start to encroach on neighbours.

Do not think you need to own a cottage in the country to have a cottage garden. Small plots of modern town houses look very good when planted in this way. Cottage gardening is enjoying great popularity today among both country and town dwellers, with the resurgent interest in the English style of gardening.

CHOICE OF PLANTS

When looking for old-fashioned perennials with which to plant beds and borders in the cottage garden there is certainly no lack of choice.

Good companions for the perennials described below would be

shrubs such as philadelphus or mock orange; lilac, *Syringa vulgaris*; flowering currant, *Ribes sanguineum*; forsythias; buddleias; ornamental quince, *Chaenomeles japonica*; old-fashioned shrub roses, including moss roses; and the mezereon, *Daphne mezereum*.

Essential climbers are climbing and rambling roses; clematis, particularly small-flowered kinds like *C. montana* and *C. alpina*; honeysuckle, *Lonicera periclymenum* and its varieties; the grape vine, *Vitis* 'Brandt'; winter jasmine, *Jasminum nudiflorum;* summer jasmine, *J. officinale*; and ornamental ivies or hedera.

Hardy annuals, grown from seed sown *in situ*, form another important group, and should include such favourites as love-in-a-mist (nigella); pot marigold (calendula); candytuft (iberis); stocks (matthiola); cornflower (centaurea); and clary (*Salvia sclarea*). Half-hardy annuals can include tobacco plant, nicotiana; geraniums or pelargoniums; verbena; and heliotrope.

Spring-flowering bulbs of all kinds make good companions for perennials, too, including all the miniature ones like scillas, muscari and crocuses. Also have some rock plants for spring colour, including aubrieta; dwarf phloxes; rock pinks or dianthus; rock roses, helianthemums; house leeks or sempervivums; and yellow alyssum, *Aylssum saxatile*.

And do not forget the popular British native plants that are available from seedsmen and nurserymen, like primroses, *Primula vulgaris*; cowslips, *Primula veris*; ox-eye daisy, *Chrysanthemum leucanthemum*; heartsease, *Viola tricolor*; and Welsh poppy, *Meconopsis cambrica*.

Well, these are a few ideas for companion plants. Let us now consider hardy perennials for the cottage-garden border. The monkshood, or *Aconitum napellus*, has hooded flowers and it should be pointed out that all parts of the plants are poisonous, so guard against this if you have children. There are several varieties but one of the best is 'Bressingham Spire' with dark violet-blue flowers.

Hollyhocks or *Althaea rosea* are very much cottage-garden perennials and their tall stems bearing rosette flowers look lovely against an old brick wall, say alongside the front door. Alternatively they are back-of-the-border plants. There are several varieties, but the best undoubtedly is 'Chater's Double', with paeonia-like double flowers in various colours, such as shades of pink, red, yellow and white.

For bright blue flowers in summer it is hard to beat *Anchusa italica* (also known as *A. azurea*). There are several varieties but very popular is 'Loddon Royalist' with the most beautiful gentian blue flowers.

Columbines or aquilegias were certainly to be found in many of the old cottage gardens. They have funnel-shaped blooms with a spur at the back, and are rather short-lived perennials so will have to be replaced every few years. Plants are easily raised from seeds, available from seedsmen, if you do not want the expense of buying new plants. Long-spurred hybrids of *A. vulgaris* probably make the best show and come in a wide range of colours. Best known are the 'McKana Hybrids' with very large flowers in many colours. I also like the variety 'Crimson Star' which has red and white blooms.

Artemisias I would certainly include in a cottage garden. I have

As one would expect of a flower arranger, this border in Sheila Macqueen's garden is crammed with enticingly cuttable flowers and foliage.

recommended several already in Chapter 6, but another you might like to try is 'Lambrook Silver'. This has grey foliage, which is much divided, and small grey flowers. It makes a nice companion for old-fashioned shrub roses with pink or red flowers.

Any of the asters or Michaelmas daisies look at home in a cottage-garden border and I have recommended several very good varieties in Chapters 5 and 6. *Aster amellus* varieties can be specially recommended and are noted for their large flowers. Probably the best-known is 'King George', an old variety with lavender blue flowers; 'Pink Zenith' produces good clear pink blooms; and 'Violet Queen' has violet coloured flowers.

Aubrieta can be used at the front of the border to trail over the path. It smothers itself with flowers in spring, after which it can be cut back fairly hard to maintain a compact habit. Choose colours which appeal to you: there are lots of good varieties including 'Bob Saunders', red-purple; 'Dr Mules', dark violet-purple; 'Greencourt Purple', semi-double purple; 'Henslow Purple', very bright purple; 'Maurice Prichard', pink; 'Red Carpet', dark red; and 'Triumphant', blue.

Dwarf and trailing campanulas or bellflowers can also be allowed to trail over the edge of the border. The *C. carpatica* varieties are excellent, like 'Chewton Joy', sky blue; 'Isobel', very deep blue; and 'Snow-sprite', pure white. *C. garganica* has sprays of blue flowers, and *C. muralis* 'Resholt Variety' produces its lavender blue flowers in profusion. I also like *Campanula* 'Stella', with blue star-like flowers in great sheets if mass planted.

Delphinium hybrids have been described in Chapter 6 and look lovely planted among shrub roses in the cottage-garden border (Fig. 15). Pinks and border carnations (dianthus) are traditional cottage-garden plants, many of the varieties being highly scented. Probably the best-known pink of all is 'Doris' with rich pink double flowers; but also well worth growing are 'Mrs Sinkins', another very old one, with double white flowers; and the old 'Sam Barlow', pink and white. Any of the border carnations on offer are worth having – just choose the colours that appeal.

Digitalis or foxgloves are recommended and you will find a selection described in Chapter 8.

Galega offiinalis, or goat's rue, is a bushy perennial of vigorous habit with globular flowers in short spikes. The best variety to grow is 'Her Majesty' which has pastel lilac blue flowers. It needs space to spread itself, but looks very much at home in a cottage garden.

Two perennials for winter colour are the Christmas rose or *Helleborus niger*, and the winter-flowering iris, *I. unguicularis*. Both have evergreen foliage. The Christmas rose produces bowl-shaped white blooms and a particularly good variety is the large-flowered 'Potter's Wheel'. For best results grow it in rich, moist soil containing plenty of humus, and in light shade. *Iris unguicularis*, on the other hand, needs a very sunny spot with well-drained, even poor soil and it does well in very chalky conditions. Best left undisturbed for as long as possible, as the plants take some time to settle down to flowering. The blooms are lavender or lilac; the variety 'Mrs Barnard' has larger blooms than the species.

To provide early and late colour in the cottage-garden border I suggest lupins, peonies (see Chapter 6) and red hot pokers (Chapter 5).

Very much an old-fashioned plant is catmint or nepeta. The usual one to grow is *N. mussinii*, which is also known as *N. × faassenii*. Due to its semi-spreading habit it is generally used as an edging plant in the border and allowed to 'soften' the edges of the path. The aromatic leaves are greyish green and in summer spikes of lavender blue flowers are produced. There is a taller variety called 'Six Hills Giant'.

Fig. 15 Delphinium hybrids look lovely planted among shrub roses in the cottage-garden border.

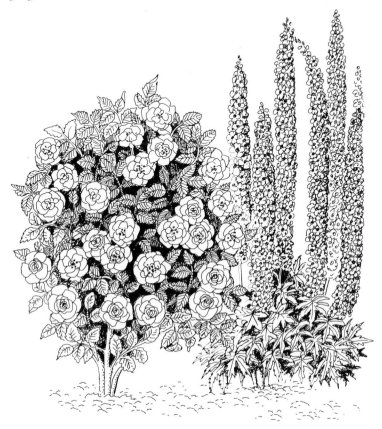

Another catmint worth growing is *N. nervosa*, a bushy plant with normal green leaves. It also bears spikes of flowers in summer, the colour being clear blue. To keep catmints neat and tidy the old stems should be cut down to the ground in the autumn.

Polemonium foliosissimum is a lovely old-fashioned border plant with upright stems which carry bowl-shaped blooms in mauve-blue. Best growth and flowering is achieved in a rich well-cultivated soil.

The genus *Primula* is huge, containing plants suitable for all parts of the garden and indeed for all styles of garden. For the cottage-garden border, though, I would recommend the 'primrose types' of primula, the low-growing ones which look lovely planted in bold groups or drifts at the front of a border. They like a fairly moist soil and do not object to a spot in partial or dappled shade. Plenty of humus in the soil will keep them happy: indeed, you will probably find that many of them sow themselves, so be careful when you carry out hoeing or hand weeding not to destroy any seedlings, for these can be carefully lifted and planted elsewhere.

What better in the English cottage garden than the true primrose, *Primula vulgaris*, a British native, with its lovely pale yellow flowers in spring. This can either be obtained as seeds from major seed companies, or as young plants from nurseries.

There are quite a few coloured primroses, in other words primulas with flowers in colours other than yellow. Some are varieties of *P. vulgaris*, and of these I can particularly recommend 'Blue Riband' with, as the name suggests, blue flowers; 'Red Velvet', which is quite new and has double flowers in rich wine red, these contrasting well with the dark green foliage, which is often flushed with purple; 'Sibthorpii', a very popular variety with lilac-mauve blooms; 'Snow Cushion', which produces pure white blooms against dark green foliage; and 'Wisley Crimson' with dark red flowers.

Coming on to other coloured primroses, undoubtedly the best known, and one that has certainly been around for a very long time, is 'Wanda', which has bright purplish red flowers in profusion. One of my great favourties is 'Garryarde Guinevere' which has beautiful bronze-flushed leaves, a marvellous background for the pink flowers, each of which has an orange centre.

For very moist soil try *P. rosea* 'Delight' with very bright pink flowers in spring. Auriculas (*P. auricula*), are charming old-fashioned plants with large pale or greyish green leaves and rounded flowers in many colours (often bi-coloured) held well above them. There are lots of varieties to choose from – I prefer simply to pick out those which appeal, when they are in flower in the garden centres.

Primula sieboldii varieties have flowers on taller stems than those of the primrose, but only attain about 15 cm (6 in) in height. There are several varieties, like 'Geisha Girl', deep pink; 'Mikado', magenta; and white 'Snowflakes'. Grow these in a cool, moist shady spot.

Good companion plants for primulas are, of course, the spring bulbs, especially the dwarf kinds, and even ferns whose new bright green unfurling fronds make a lovely foil for primulas.

Sidalceas are a good choice for the cottage garden border and I grow varieties of *S. malviflora*. They produce wide funnel-shaped blooms (mallow-like, as its name implies) in various shades of pink. Look out for the following varieties: 'Croftway Red', very deep pink; 'Mrs Alderson', rose pink; 'Rose Queen', rose pink; and 'William Smith', a lovely shade of salmon pink.

You must try to find a place in the cottage-garden border for a group or two of verbascums or mulleins. Several have been described in Chapter 6, including 'Gainsborough' which is a great favourite with many people.

Finally, no cottage garden would be complete without some violets, species and varieties of viola. These can be allowed to form carpets at the front of the border, and you may find that they seed themselves. *V. cornuta* has dark lavender flowers, which are quite large. There is a white variety named 'Alba', and a lovely light blue one called 'Boughton Blue'. *V. labradorica* 'Purpurea' has purple-flushed foliage, which makes a beautiful background for the mauve flowers.

Viola obliqua (also known as *V. cucullata*), has flowers which range from violet to white. There is also a deep pink variety named 'Rubra'. *V. odorata* is the European sweet violet, with flowers in shades of purple, or they may be white. There are several named varieties, including 'Coeur d'Alsace', deep pink; 'Czar', dark violet-purple; and 'Princess of Wales' with deep violet blooms.

Varieties derived from *Viola tricolor*, or heartsease, include 'Irish Molly', a very old favourite with copper-yellow flowers; 'Maggie Mott', pale mauve; 'Norah Leigh', lavender blue; and 'Jackanapes', yellow and deep bluish purple, old but still very popular.

It is best to remove dead flowers of violas to ensure that more follow. Also propagate regularly to maintain a succession of young plants. Cuttings of basal shoots, without flowers, can be easily rooted in summer in a cold frame.

CHAPTER 8

THE SHADY BORDER

Gardeners with shady borders often think they have a problem – that nothing will grow in such conditions. This is far from the truth: indeed I would go so far as to say that a shady area is a great advantage as it allows one to grow the wide range of shade-loving perennials.

Some borders may be shaded for only part of the day, say by the house or other buildings. Others may have dappled shade produced by trees, resembling woodland conditions. In some gardens there may be, in fact, an area of woodland. In all of these situations shade-loving plants will thrive.

There are soil conditions to consider, though, before buying shade-loving plants. In some shady areas the soil is dry, particularly in the summer, perhaps caused by nearby trees taking up most of the moisture. In other areas of shade the soil may be steadily moist, in other words not prone to drying out in the summer.

There are plants to suit both situations and the right ones must be chosen for successful results. The easiest area to establish is shade with moist soil; it is a bit more difficult establishing plants in shade with dry soil and there are fewer to choose from.

A SHADY BORDER WITH DRY SOIL

This should be well prepared before planting by digging deeply (tree roots permitting) and adding plenty of organic matter (see Chapter 2). This will help to retain moisture in the summer. After planting it is recommended that the plants are permanently mulched with organic matter, again to help conserve moisture during dry periods (see Chapter 4).

You may want to form a framework of shrubs among which you can plant your perennials. The following shrubs are particularly recommended for dry shaded soils:

Aucuba japonica, the spotted laurel with evergreen yellow-mottled leaves in varieties 'Crotonoides' and 'Maculata'; *Ilex aquifolium* 'J.C. van Tol', a variety of common holly with almost spineless leaves and heavy crops of red berries in autumn/winter; *Ruscus aculeatus*, the butcher's broom, with evergreen spiny foliage and large red berries; and *Skimmia japonica*, an evergreen with cream flowers and red berries (grow both male and female plants to ensure crops of berries).

There are several excellent perennials which flower in the spring and these could be grouped together in one part of the border, perhaps in association with spring-flowering shrubs like forsythia and *Ribes* (flowering currant) and spring bulbs, which do not mind partial shade.

The pulmonarias are among my favourites for spring colour. There are several varieties of *P. saccharata* including 'Sissinghurst White', white flowers; *P. saccharata argentea* with silvery foliage and blue flowers; 'Bowles Red', red blooms; 'Highdown', deep blue; and 'Pink Dawn', pink.

You could combine with the pulmonarias London pride or *Saxifraga* × *urbium* with its neat evergreen foliage and dainty sprays of palest pink blooms; and the barrenworts or epimediums which make excellent ground cover if mass planted. There are lots to choose from including *E. cantabrigensis* with brown-orange flowers; *E. macranthum*, pink, and its variety 'Rose Queen', deep pink; *E. perralderianum* 'Frohnleiten', golden yellow; *E. rubrum*, red; *E. sulphureum*, pale yellow; *E. warleyense,* orangey flowers; *E. youngianum* 'Niveum', white; and *E. youngianum* 'Roseum', pink. In most epimediums the spring foliage is very attractive, sometimes flushed with bronze. In the autumn, too, it often takes on attractive tints before it starts to die down.

Also flowering in spring is the rampant ground-cover plant *Lamiastrum luteum* 'Variegatum', the yellow archangel. Only grow this if you want to cover a large area quickly, although it should be said that it is easy enough to dig out if it starts to encroach on other plants. It has the most beautiful silver-splashed foliage and spikes of yellow flowers.

Related to lamiastrum but nowhere near as vigorous are the ground-cover lamiums or dead nettles. *L. maculatum* 'Beacon Silver' is a superb plant with silvery white foliage and pink flowers. I also like 'Roseum' with pink flowers. Both quickly cover the ground but are not invasive. I like to grow the lamiums and lamiastrums around spring-flowering shrubs and trees.

Also coming into flower in spring but continuing into summer are the symphytums, again good ground-cover plants. *S. grandiflorum* is the best known with cream-white flowers; its variety 'Hidcote' is more attractive in my opinion with light blue-pink blooms. Sprays of deep red flowers are produced by *S. rubrum* which is a fairly scarce plant but offered by some specialist nurseries.

Taking the display into summer are the foxgloves or digitalis with their tall spires of tubular flowers, often attractively spotted. There are several hybrids available like the 'Excelsior' hybrids with flowers in many colours. I also like some of the species, particularly *D. ambigua* with pale yellow flowers which show up well in shade; and *D. mertonensis* with bright pink blooms.

One could easily be put off *Iris foetidissima*, the stinking gladwyn, by its names; but don't be, for it's well worth growing for its lilac flowers which are followed in autumn by seed pods which eventually spit open to reveal bright orange seeds. It has evergreen foliage and ideally should be planted alongside shrubs with bright autumn leaves and with perennials like epimediums.

Finally another ground-cover plant – one of the crane's-bills, *Geranium macrorrhizum* 'Album', which has aromatic foliage and a long succession of white flowers in spring and summer.

A SHADY BORDER WITH MOIST SOIL

The gardener with these conditions is indeed fortunate for they allow you to grow some truly beautiful plants, including choice woodland perennials. Not much initial preparation is needed but most plants would appreciate plenty of peat or leafmould being dug into the soil before planting, plus a permanent mulch of these materials.

Again, plants could be grouped according to seasons, in association with shrubs and other plants.

Any planting scheme really needs a permanent framework of shrubs and the following can be recommended for moist soils in shade:

Fatsia japonica, an evergreen with large hand-shaped leaves and white flowers in autumn; *Hamamelis mollis*, the Chinese witch hazel, with yellow flowers in winter (a good variety is 'Pallida'), needs acid or lime-free soil); *Hydrangea macrophylla*, the Hortensia and lace-cap varieties, with blue, pink, red or white flowers in late summer (blue flowers on acid soils, pink on limy or alkaline soils); *Pernettya mucronata*, an evergreen with pink or red berries (plant male and female plants), should be grown in acid soil; and rhododendrons and azaleas, evergreen and deciduous, flowering in spring (some in winter) and early summer, in all colours and sizes, acid or lime-free soil being essential for their survival.

One of my favourite schemes for spring includes bergenias, ajugas, metensias, brunneras, omphalodes and an ornamental grass, milium. The bergenias are excellent ground-cover plants, with large rounded evergreen leaves which sometimes take on colourful tints in autumn and winter. In spring the sprays of flowers appear and last for many weeks. There are lots of varieties to choose from including 'Admiral',

(*Left*) Ladies mantle, *Alchemilla mollis,* provides a soft green foil for the blue spires of delphiniums and frothy pink roses.

Deep blue anchusas (*right*), poppies, irises and a mixture of Russell lupins give this planting a particularly cottagey atmosphere.

red flowers; 'Ballawley', rose red; 'Bressingham Salmon'; 'Bressing-ham White'; *B. cordifolia purpurea*, pink blooms and purplish leaves; 'Pugsley's Pink'; and the gorgeous 'Silberlicht' with white flowers.

Ajuga reptans varieties are prostrate ground-cover plants and popular-ly known as bugles. The ones to look out for are 'Burgundy Glow' with multicoloured foliage and pale blue flowers; 'Purpurea' with reddish purple foliage and bright blue flowers; 'Multicolor' with colourful foliage and blue flowers; and 'Variegata' with cream and green variegated foliage and blue flowers.

Mertensia echioides is a lovely plant with sprays of bright blue flowers, and so, too, is *Brunnera macrophylla* 'Langtrees' which is like a large perennial forget-me-not. *Omphalodes verna* also resembles a forget-me-not, again with the most beautiful blue flowers. Among these blue flowers I like to plant the golden-leaved grass *Milium effusum* 'Aureum', which does best in partial shade.

A really beautiful summer group can be created in moist shade with hostas for foliage (Fig. 16), astilbes, primulas, meconopsis and ferns.

There are a large number of hostas or plantain lilies to choose from. They have large bold deciduous foliage which comes in all shades of green and many variegations. There are lots of good new varieties as well as several old favourites. All make excellent ground cover. The following can be recommended (all produce flowers in the summer, in shades of mauve, lilac, white, etc):

Fig. 16 A lovely combination for a shady border with moist soil – hostas and astilbes.

Green-leaved hostas – 'Big Daddy', blue-green; *H. fortunei*, greyish green; 'Halcyon', silvery grey; 'Honeybells'; *H. lancifolia; H. planta-ginea* 'Grandiflora'; 'Royal Standard'; *H. sieboldiana* 'Elegans', blue-green; and *H. tardiana*, also blue-green. Gold-leaved hostas include *H. fortunei* 'Aurea'; 'Gold Edger'; 'Gold Standard'; 'Golden Medallion'; 'Golden Prayers'; 'Piedmont Gold'; and 'Sun Power'. Among good variegated hostas are *H. crispula; H. decorata; H. fortunei* 'Aureo-marginata; *H. fortunei* 'Picta'; 'Francee'; 'Frances Williams'; 'Ginko Craig'; 'Ground Master'; 'Shade Fanfare'; 'Thomas Hogg'; *H. undulata* 'Medio-variegata'; and *H. ventricosa* 'Variegata'.

Varieties of *Astilbe × arendsii* can be grown in partial shade – they do like some sun. In summer beautiful feathery plumes of flowers are produced. There are many varieties like 'Amethyst', lilac-rose; 'Fanal', deep red; 'Ostrich Plume', coral pink; and 'Snowdrift', white.

Of the primulas I would recommend mainly the candelabra types with tall flower stalks carrying the blooms in tiers. I can recommend *P. bulleyana*, orange blooms; *P. florindae*, pale yellow, scented; *P. japonica* 'Miller's Crimson', red; *P. japonica* 'Postford White', white; *P. pulverulenta*, bright red; *P. sikkimensis*, pale yellow, scented.

The meconopsis recommended for this group are the blue poppies, which need acid or lime-free soil. The best-known is *M. betonicifolia*. Then there is *M. grandis*, and *M. × sheldonii* 'Branklyn' with exceptionally large flowers.

Plant ferns among all these flowering plants to act as a cool green foil. There are lots to choose from like *Athyrium filix-femina* with fresh green, deeply divided fronds; *Dryopteris filix-mas*, also with deeply divided fronds, evergreen in mild parts of the country; *Phyllitis scolopendrium* with long tongue-shaped, bright green fronds, generally evergreen; and *Polystichum setiferum*, a truly beautiful fern with evergreen fronds which look particularly lovely when they are unfurling in the spring.

There are many other plants for moist shade including the goat's beard or *Aruncus sylvester* which will thrive in partial shade, producing in summer tall plumes of cream flowers. It looks particularly lovely associated with *Rodgersia pinnata* varieties which are grown for their bold foliage. One of my favourites is 'Superba' which has beautiful bronze-purple foliage and pink flowers. 'Irish Bronze' is also to be recommended, this, too, having bronze foliage and pink blooms. *R. pinnata* itself has green foliage and cream-pink blooms.

A beautiful little ground-cover plant for massing around shrubs and larger plants is the woodruff, *Asperula odorata* (also known as *Galium odoratum*), a British native. It carries whorls of bright green leaves and tiny white fragrant flowers. When mass planted in bold drifts or groups it produces a pleasing effect.

The masterwort or *Astrantia major* produces starry greenish-pink flowers in summer and is a popular woodland plant. There are several good varieties: 'Rosea' with pink flowers and 'Variegata' with variegated leaves and green flowers.

An unusual plant is *Cautleya robusta* which gives an exotic touch to a woodland, so it is not in keeping if you are aiming for a typical English woodland scene. It looks more at home clustered around rho-dodendrons and azaleas. The large leaves look like those of the tropical cannas or Indian shot and in summer sturdy spikes of yellow flowers are produced. Partial shade and plenty of moisture suit this plant.

The bugbanes or cimicifugas are tall, very graceful plants which enjoy light shade and moist humus-rich soil. Leave the plants well alone once planted for they do not like root disturbance. The ferny leaves are attractive and above these appear in summer spikes of white flowers. Two species are popular: *C. cordifolia* (also known as *C. americana*) and *C. racemosa* which is popularly known as the black snake root.

Lily of the valley, or *Convallaria majalis,* is a great favourite for shady moist places with its sweetly fragrant white flowers in spring. There are several varieties including 'Plena' with double flowers, the pink-flowered 'Rosea' and 'Variegata' whose leaves are striped with green and yellow. Lily of the valley will quickly colonize an area if it is happy but it never becomes a nuisance. Ensure there is plenty of peat or leafmould in the soil and that the ground never dries out. Mulch annually with peat or leafmould once the leaves have died down. This will help to conserve moisture.

The erythroniums are woodland plants of a bulbous nature and flower in the spring. A very popular one is a hybrid of *E. tuolumnense* called 'Pagoda' with nodding lily-like yellow flowers, each with a central brown zone, and attractive bronze leaves. Moist soil is absolutely essential and it should be well supplied with organic matter like peat or leafmould. It is best to leave these plants alone as they dislike disturbance, but if you have to move them the best time is when the foliage has died down, some time after flowering.

The dropwort, or *Filipendula hexapetala* 'Grandiflora' (also known as *F. vulgaris*) is related to the spiraeas and has similar large fluffy flower heads in summer. The creamy white flowers are scented and show up well against the luxuriant ferny foliage.

An attractive ground-cover plant is × *Heucherella tiarelloides* which is a cross between heuchera and tiarella. It has attractive foliage and in summer bears tall sprays of tiny salmon pink bell-shaped blooms.

Solomon's seal, *Polygonatum multiflorum*, is a woodland plant with a lot of character. It has arching stems which carry, in early summer, rows of white bell-shaped flowers. It is a British native plant and although generally listed under the above name it is, correctly, a hybrid of *P. multiflorum* and *P. odoratum*. It is an easy-going plant and likes a good root run. Solomon's seal is very prone to attacks by the caterpillars of the Solomon's seal sawfly, which can quickly strip plants of their leaves. Dust the plants with derris insecticide.

The next plant I want to recommend is the false Solomon's seal, *Smilacina racemosa*. This is a true woodland plant, too, and revels in a moist shady spot. It produces upright stems densely clothed in attractive lanceolate leaves. The flowers, carried in arching sprays during late spring or early summer, are creamy white and pleasantly scented. It is a slow grower and once planted should be left undisturbed.

Finally a wood lily, also known as wake robin, *Trillium grandiflorum*. It carries in spring and early summer three-petalled white flowers which, as they age, become flushed with pink. Make sure you add plenty of peat or leafmould to the soil before planting and then plant in a bold drift between shrubs. The young shoots are very prone to slug damage so put down some slug pellets in the spring as the plants are coming into growth.

CHAPTER 9

THE HOT
DRY BORDER

From shade we move to sun. But more than just sun – a very hot and dry situation, with sun all day long and perhaps a gravelly soil which is extremely well drained and dries out rapidly in summer.

Perhaps this is typical of a very sheltered corner in your garden which acts as a sun trap; or maybe it is a south-facing bank or slope.

Unless you choose the right plants this can be an extremely difficult situation to keep looking attractive. But with suitable plants you can transform such an area into a 'little bit of Mediterranean maquis'.

Suitable plants do indeed include some of Mediterranean origin, but also from other parts of the world, too – plants which grow naturally in very poor soil conditions and intense sun. Many of the plants which grow in these conditions have woolly or silver foliage, while others may have a succulent habit of growth with the ability to store water to tide them over long dry periods.

If you have an arid area in your garden you should not try to alter it too much but go along with it. For instance, once the area is planted it would be appropriate to cover the soil with a layer of shingle or stone chippings, no more than 2.5 cm (1 in) deep, to resemble the stony or rough, rocky terrain from which the plants originate. This will also benefit the plants, for a 'mineral mulch' will help to conserve soil moisture during hot dry periods. And, of course, it will suppress the growth of annual weeds, so cutting down on maintenance.

I do not see any point in needlessly giving the plants a hard time, so prepare the soil thoroughly before planting so that they establish quickly and grow well. Carry out double digging if possible and certainly incorporate plenty of bulky organic matter such as thoroughly rotted farmyard manure, garden compost, leafmould, peat or pulverized bark (see Chapter 2). Then before planting work into the surface a general-purpose fertilizer. Each spring a topdressing of fertilizer should be given. If possible carry out regular watering during dry periods in summer. All of this will help your plants to grow well – they will be far superior to the stunted specimens one often sees in the wild.

As with most planting schemes you should use some shrubs as a basis around which to plan your border, ideally ensuring that the perennials you choose associate well, or look good, with their woody companions. There are several shrubs which revel in hot dry conditions and I can recommend the following:

Artemisia arborescens, wormwood, silvery leaves; Cistus, rock rose, pink, red, purple or white flowers, evergreen; Colutea arborescens, bladder senna, yellow flowers; Cytisus × beanii, broom, yellow flowers; Cytisus × kewensis, broom, pale yellow; Genista hispanica, Spanish gorse, yellow, spiny; Genista lydia , broom, yellow flowers; Helianthemum nummularium, rock rose, many colours; Lavandula officinalis, lavender, grey-blue flowers, grey foliage; Potentilla fruticosa, shrubby cinquefoil, yellow, orange, red, pink or white flowers; Rosmarinus officinalis, rosemary, mauve flowers, evergreen aromatic foliage; Santolina chamaecyparissus, cotton lavender, yellow flowers, silver woolly evergreen foliage; Spartium junceum, Spanish broom, yellow flowers; Ulex europaeus 'Plenus', double-flowered gorse, yellow flowers, very spiny, needs acid soil; and Yucca filamentosa, Adam's needle, bold sword-like foliage, cream flowers.

A CHOICE OF PERENNIALS

Now let's consider some suitable perennials for hot dry situations. Again, wherever possible, try to create some pleasing plant associations. For instance I like to grow together Anthemis cupaniana and herbaceous potentilla hybrids. The anthemis forms a carpet of silver foliage and is quite a good ground-cover plant. However in a hard winter the growth may die back, so then it will need cutting back in early spring before it starts into growth. Anthemis flowers for a very long period in the summer, bearing masses of daisy-like flowers which are white with yellow centres. It flourishes even in the poorest of conditions.

The herbaceous potentilla hybrids provide bright colour in the summer with their small dog-rose-like flowers. Some of the popular varieties include 'Gibson's Scarlet', which bears brilliant scarlet blooms; 'Monsieur Rouillard' with double crimson flowers; 'William Rollisson' with brilliant orange semi-double blooms; 'Yellow Queen', deep yellow blooms set against attractive silvery leaves; 'Blazeaway' with single orange-red flowers; and 'Flamenco' with single brilliant red blooms.

Another combination which I like consists of drifts of Centranthus ruber, or red valerian, and Elymus arenarius, the lyme grass – a study in pink and grey.

The centranthus is a bushy plant with grey-green, rather fleshy leaves. During the summer it flowers for a very long period, bearing heads of deep pink or reddish blooms. If you want deep red flowers then plant the variety 'Atrococcineus'. The lyme grass is an extremely beautiful ornamental grass, but it has one drawback – it is excessively vigorous and can rapidly colonize a large area of ground. Of course, in some places, such as difficult banks, perhaps with loose sandy soil, this can be a great advantage as the grass will stabilize the soil. The lyme grass has broad leaves in a beautiful shade of blue-grey and in summer it bears spikes of flowers in the same colour.

Another plant association which I can recommend is *Zauschneria californica* or *Z. cana* and *Phlomis viscosa*.

Zauschneria californica is not too hardy, unfortunately, and could be killed in a hard winter. Therefore it is recommended only for milder parts of the country. During the summer and autumn it produces sprays of scarlet trumpet-shaped flowers, which are rather like those of fuchsias, hence the common name of Californian fuchsia. *Z. cana* is also worth looking out for as it has silver-grey foliage which makes a superb background for the scarlet fuchsia-like flowers. Again it is not too hardy and may be killed in a severe winter.

Phlomis viscosa has big heart-shaped leaves which have rather a rough texture. In the summer flower stems appear which carry whorls of yellow blooms. The seed heads which follow are attractive and therefore I generally leave them until they become tatty later in the year. Some people cut and dry them for use in winter flower arrangements. These two plants, then, zauschneria and phlomis, contrast beautifully in flower and foliage colour and shape.

I am very fond of the eryngiums and would certainly include in a hot dry area some of the more unusual species. *Eryngium agavifolium* has a very exotic appearance, though it is fairly tender and might not survive a very cold winter. It needs plenty of space as it produces massive spine-edged sword-like leaves up to 1.5 m (5 ft) long. In the summer it produces 2 m (6 ft) high flower stems bearing white blooms.

Eryngium bourgatii is a dwarf plant with deeply cut greyish green foliage attractively marked with grey-white. Blue flowers, each surrounded with a collar of long prickly bracts, appear in the summer and are very attractive. This is far more hardy than *E. agavifolium* and indeed is an easily grown perennial. It would look good in association with herbaceous potentilla hybrids or with Californian fuchsias.

Another easy-going eryngium, again of dwarf habit, is *E. variifolium* which is most effective when planted in large groups or drifts. It forms a neat rosette of rounded spiny toothed leaves which are veined with white. In the summer grey-blue flowers, each with a pale spiny 'collar', are produced.

A charming *Rosa rubrifolia* forms the
background to this corner planting
with its foxgloves, yellow phlomis
and purple Canterbury bells.

Fig. 17 A new plant introduction
suitable for the hot dry border is
the creamy-yellow *Phygelius aequalis*
'Yellow Trumpet'.

Do you like thistles? If so, try *Morina longifolia,* though be warned it has a tidy rosette of very prickly green leaves, so make sure you plant it in a position where it will not cause any harm! In the summer the plant produces tall flower stems which carry whorls of white and pink, tubular hooded flowers. This is another plant that's not very hardy and so only really suited to the milder parts of the country.

Although it has a somewhat shrubby habit of growth *Phygelius capensis* is often treated as a herbaceous plant, having its stems cut down in the autumn or winter. It can also be grown up a wall if desired, when it will attain a height of about 2 m (6 ft) and have a shrubby habit of growth. It would certainly relish a warm sheltered south-facing wall. Phygelius has a very long flowering season – it starts around mid-summer and only stops in the autumn when the frosts commence. It has masses of tubular flowers, bright red, each with a yellow throat. It is also worth looking out for a form known as *P. capensis* 'Coccineus' which is probably a bit brighter in colour and each flower has more yellow in the throat.

A new plant introduction from the famous Bressingham Gardens is *Phygelius aequalis* 'Yellow Trumpet' (Fig. 17). This is quite a leafy plant, with bright green foliage; flowering starts in mid-summer and continues well into the autumn. The tubular flowers are creamy yellow. It needs shelter, maximum sun and perfect drainage. Bressingham Gardens recommend protecting the crown of the plant in winter.

Among the succulent-type plants for a hot dry area are the sedums or stonecrops. There are lots of species and quite honestly any would be suitable. They grow in the poorest of conditions and flower profusely in the summer.

However, my personal choice would certainly include *Sedum aizoon* 'Aurantiacum' with deep yellow flowers and attractive reddish stems. The flowers are followed by attractive red seed pods. You could grow the species itself, *S. aizoon,* which has yellow flowers, but it is not as attractive as its variety.

Another sedum I would not be without is *S. telephium* 'Munstead Red' (which, as luck would have it, contrasts superbly with *S. aizoon* 'Aurantiacum'). It has deep green leaves which are flushed with purple and in late summer it produces flat heads of brownish red flowers which last for many weeks. Some people may find these flowers rather sombre, but this effect is relieved by suitable companion plants. Try it with phygelius, for instance, or with zauschneria. It is also a good companion for silver- or grey-leaved shrubs.

This, then, is my choice of plants for a hot dry situation. With these you will have colour and interest throughout the year.

· CHAPTER 10 ·

THE CLAY BORDER

Many people have gardens on clay and from the letters I receive it seems that they feel they want to give up gardening altogether.

I know the feeling, for I once had a new garden on really thick stiff clay which held water on the surface whenever it rained but dried out and became baked as hard as a rock during hot weather in summer. Nevertheless I got to grips with it and certainly managed to grow a very wide range of plants, including many perennials or herbaceous plants.

Indeed, if you can get a clay soil to drain well, so that surplus water does not lie on the surface but disappears quickly to lower levels, you have a really good soil for plants. A clay soil is generally fertile and during drought conditions remains moist lower down, even though the surface may dry out, so plants continue to grow.

In a really well-drained clay soil one can even grow many of the silver- or grey-leaved perennials which are generally thought of as being suitable only for light sandy or gravelly soils.

I will describe how I tackled my plot of clay soil and hope that this will give you some ideas and, most importantly, encouragement.

The garden was on really thick yellow clay – indeed the site was formerly a brickworks! Water laid on the surface during the winter for weeks at a time and when working my boots literally got stuck in the soil – it was just like plasticine.

Desperate measures were called for so the first job was double digging to two depths of the spade: just a little at a time as it was really heavy work. At the same time I placed a thick layer of straw in the bottom of each trench to help improve the drainage. Bales of straw are cheap to buy from a local agricultural merchant. It is best to compost the straw before use, but I must admit that I used it in the fresh state.

It was quite unbelievable how much the drainage was improved by the addition of straw. I left the ground roughly dug over one winter after applying to the surface a generous amount of horticultural gypsum. This helps to break down the surface soil and takes out the stickiness so that in the spring as the soil is becoming drier it can be more easily prepared for sowing and planting.

Although it is still available, and relatively cheap, horticultural gypsum has been largely superseded by proprietary soil conditioners which have exactly the same effect on clay soils. They are based on various materials, including seaweed and farmyard manure. Calcified seaweed is probably one of the best known. A range of soil conditioners can be bought from any good garden centre and should be used according to the manufacturer's instructions. Generally they are sprinkled on the surface after digging, or incorporated into the topsoil during digging.

In the spring following digging I then worked into the top 30 cm (12 in) a good quantity of horticultural grit, the type used in potting composts. This further helped to improve drainage.

Unfortunately the builders removed all the topsoil and carted it away so I had to buy in a load – I chose a light sandy topsoil! It should be said, though, that there is no need to buy in topsoil if you already have a good depth in your garden – about 30 cm (12 in).

This treatment solved my drainage problems and I successfully grew a wide range of plants.

In some gardens, though, the only way to improve drainage is to lay land drain pipes to a soakaway. This used to be a formidable task as one had to dig deep, wide trenches to lay bulky clay drain pipes on aggregate. Land drainage is far easier today, though, as there is available a DIY system of narrow plastic land-drain pipes which are easily laid in slit trenches, so minimizing soil disturbance. They need only be laid about 25 cm (10 in) deep and come in long lengths so they are quick to lay. To be effective over a large area – say a complete garden – the drainage pipes should be spaced at about 90 cm (3 ft) intervals. You will need to dig a soakaway at the lowest point of the garden. This is simply a deep hole filled with hardcore then topped with shingle and finally soil. The average small garden will need a soakaway at least 1.2 m (4 ft) deep.

Another way to improve the drainage of clay soils is to cultivate as I have explained above but to raise the borders by about 15 cm (6 in) or so. This is achieved by shifting the soil until the borders are higher than the surrounding land. To some extent this is achieved by double digging and adding plenty of bulky organic matter like straw or garden compost.

Once you have solved the problem of drainage you should not neglect clay soils. Regular applications of bulky organic matter like garden compost, farmyard manure, peat, pulverized bark, etc, either dug in or used as a mulch, will continue to improve growing conditions.

SUITABLE PLANTS FOR CLAY SOILS

Now let us consider suitable border perennials for clay soil. As you can see below there is a surprisingly wide range to choose from. All of those listed have been described elsewhere in the book and I have found that they do well on clay soil provided it is improved as outlined earlier. You will see that some of the plants in this list are also recommended elsewhere in the book for dry or very well-drained situations. These, however, are also suitable for clay soils because they are exceedingly adaptable.

Achillea filipendulina 'Gold Plate'
Achillea 'Moonshine'
Achillea ptarmica 'The Pearl'
Aconitum napellus 'Bressingham Spire'
Ajuga reptans varieties
Alchemilla mollis
Aruncus sylvester
Aster acris
Aster amellus varieties
Aster novae-angliae varieties
Aster novi-belgii varieties
Astilbe × *arendsii* varieties
Astrantia major
Athyrium filix-femina
Campanula carpatica varieties
Campanula glomerata varieties
Campanula lactiflora
Campanula latifolia
Campanula persicifolia
Campanula species, dwarf
Centaurea dealbata
Centranthus ruber
Chelone barbata
Convallaria majalis
Coreopsis verticillata 'Grandiflora'
Crambe cordifolia
Digitalis ambigua
Digitalis hybrids
Digitalis mertonensis
Doronicum varieties
Dryopteris filix-mas
Echinops ritro
Epimedium species
Erigeron hybrids
Eupatorium purpureum
  'Atropurpureum'

Euphorbia epithymoides
Euphorbia griffithii 'Fireglow'
Euphorbia sikkimensis
Filipendula hexapetala 'Grandiflora'
Gentiana asclepiadea
Geranium endressii varieties
Geranium macrorrhizum 'Album'
Geranium sanguineum
Helenium hybrids
Heliopsis patula
Helleborus niger
Helleborus orientalis
Hemerocallis varieties
Hosta species and varieties
Inula 'Golden Beauty'
Iris foetidissima
Iris germanica varieties
Iris pallida 'Variegata'
Iris unguicularis
Lamiastrum luteum 'Variegatum'
Lychnis chalcedonica
Lychnis coronaria varieties
Lychnis viscaria 'Splendens Plena'
Lysimachia clethroides
Lysimachia punctata
Lythrum salicaria varieties
Lythrum virgatum 'The Rocket'
Macleaya cordata
Mertensia echioides
Oenothera glaber
Oenothera 'Highlight'
Omphalodes verna
Phlomis viscosa
Phyllitis scolopendrium
Physalis franchetii
Physostegia virginiana

Polemonium foliosissimum
Polygonum affine
Polygonum bistorta 'Superbum'
Polystichum setiferum
Potentilla hybrids
Primula, primrose types
Primula species, e.g. candelabra types
Prunella grandiflora (syn. *P. webbiana*)
Pulmonaria angustifolia
Pulmonaria saccharata varieties
Rodgersia pinnata varieties

Rudbeckia deamii
Rudbeckia fulgida 'Goldsturm'
Salvia superba varieties
Saxifraga × *urbium*
Sidalcea varieties
Solidago varieties
Stachys lanata 'Silver Carpet'
Stachys macrantha 'Superba'
Tradescantia virginiana varieties
Trollius × *cultorum* varieties

Rich contrasting ·colours from lupins, pyrethrums and a selection of violas form the main interest of this border in a Hampshire garden (*above*).

Moisture-loving perennials from hostas and ferns to mimulus and Japanese primulas revel in this streamside situation (*right*). Most might fail elsewhere.

APPENDIX

AT-A-GLANCE GUIDE TO BORDER PLANTS

All of the perennial plants described in previous chapters are listed here, with details of height (when in flower or fully grown); number of plants needed per square metre (square yard) when planting in groups; and flowering period.

Name	Height in cm (in)		No per m² (sq yd)	Flowering period
Acanthus longifolius	75	(30)	3–4	Mid-summer to early autumn
Acanthus spinosus	120	(48)	3–4	Mid-summer to early autumn
Achillea filipendulina 'Gold Plate'	150	(60)	4	Early summer to early autumn
Achillea 'Moonshine'	60	(24)	4–5	Early to late summer
Achillea ptarmica 'The Pearl'	75	(30)	3	Early to late summer
Aconitum napellus 'Bressingham Spire'	90	(36)	5–7	Mid- to late summer
Adonis amurensis 'Fukujukai'	25	(10)	5–6	Late winter to early spring
Agapanthus campanulatus 'Isis'	75	(30)	4–5	Late summer to early autumn
Agapanthus 'Headbourne Hybrids'	90	(36)	4	Mid- to late summer
Ajuga reptans varieties	10	(4)	5–6	Late spring to early summer
Alchemilla mollis	45	(18)	4–5	Early to late summer
Althaea rosea 'Chaters Double Mixed'	200	(80)	5	Early to late summer

Name	Height in cm (in)		No per m² (sq yd)	Flowering period
Anaphalis triplinervis 'Summer Snow'	30	(12)	3	Mid-summer to early autumn
Anchusa italica 'Loddon Royalist'	90	(36)	4	Late spring to mid-summer
Anemone hybrida varieties	60	(24)	5–7	Late summer to mid-autumn
Anthemis cupaniana	30	(12)	5	Late spring to late summer
Anthemis tinctoria varieties	75	(30)	4–5	Early to late summer
Aquilegia varieties	75	(30)	5	Early to late summer
Artemisia lactiflora	120	(48)	3–4	Late summer to early autumn
Artemisia 'Lambrook Silver'	90	(36)	4	Late summer to early autumn
Artemisia ludoviciana	120	(48)	3–4	Early autumn
Aruncus sylvester	150	(60)	3	Early to mid-summer
Asperula odorata	15	(6)	5	Late spring to early summer
Aster acris	75	(30)	5	Late summer to early autumn
Aster amellus varieties	60–90	(24–36)	5	Late summer to mid-autumn
Aster novae-angliae varieties	120	(48)	4	Early to mid-autumn
Aster novi-belgii tall	60–90	(24–36)	5	Early to
dwarf	30	(12)	5	mid-autumn
Astilbe × arendsii varieties	60–75	(24–30)	4–5	Early to late summer
Astrantia major	90	(36)	4	Early to late summer
Athyrium filix-femina	75	(30)	3	—
Aubrieta varieties	10–15	(4–6)	5	Early to late spring
Bergenia varieties	30	(12)	3–4	Mid- to late spring
Brunnera macrophylla 'Langtrees'	40	(15)	4	Mid-spring to early summer

Name	Height in cm (in)	No per m² (sq yd)	Flowering period
Campanula carpatica varieties	15–20 (6–8)	6–7	Early to late summer
Campanula glomerata varieties	30–75 (12–30)	4–5	Early to late summer
Campanula lactiflora	120 (48)	4	Early to late summer
Campanula latifolia	100 (40)	4	Early to late summer
Campanula persicifolia	75–100 (30–40)	5	Early to late summer
Campanula species, dwarf	10–15 (4–6)	5–6	Early to late summer
Cautleya robusta	120 (48)	4	Mid-summer to early autumn
Centaurea dealbata	60 (24)	4	Early to late summer
Centranthus ruber	75 (30)	5	Early summer to early autumn
Chelone barbata	90 (36)	5	Early summer to early autumn
Chrysanthemum maximum varieties	75–90 (30–36)	5	Mid-summer to early autumn
Cimicifuga cordifolia	120 (48)	4	Late summer to mid-autumn
Cimicifuga racemosa	120–150 (48–60)	4	Late summer to early autumn
Clematis heracleifolia	100 (40)	3	Mid-summer to early autumn
Convallaria majalis	15–20 (6–8)	9	Mid- to late spring
Coreopsis verticillata 'Grandiflora'	60 (24)	5	Mid-summer to early autumn
Cortaderia selloana varieties	200–240 (80–96)	1	Early to mid-autumn
Crambe cordifolia	180 (72)	3	Late spring to mid-summer
Crocosmia hybrids	60–75 (24–30)	7	Mid-summer to early autumn
Cynara cardunculus	200 (80)	2–3	Mid- to late summer
Cynara scolymus	200 (80)	2–3	Mid- to late summer

Name	Height in cm (in)	No per m² (sq yd)	Flowering period
Delphinium hybrids, tall	150–200 (60–80)	4–5	Early to late summer
Dianthus hybrids	15–30 (6–12)	4–5	Early summer to early autumn
Dicentra eximia	20 (8)	5	Mid-spring to early summer
Dicentra formosa	45 (18)	4	Mid-spring
Dicentra spectabilis	60 (24)	4	Mid-spring
Dictamnus fraxinella	75 (30)	5	Early to late summer
Digitalis ambigua	60 (24)	5	Early to late summer
Digitalis hybrids	100–150 (40–60)	5	Early to mid-summer
Digitalis mertonensis	75 (30)	5	Early to late summer
Doronicum varieties	30–60 (12–24)	5	Early to late spring
Dryopteris filix-mas	60 (24)	3	—
Echinacea purpurea varieties	90 (36)	4–5	Mid-summer to early autumn
Echinops ritro	100 (40)	4	Early summer to early autumn
Elymus arenarius	60 (24)	3	Mid- to late summer
Epimedium species	25–30 (10–12)	5	Mid- to late spring
Eremurus hybrids	200–240 (80–96)	1	Early to mid-summer
Erigeron hybrids	45–60 (18–24)	5	Mid- to late summer
Eryngium agavifolium	200 (80)	1	Mid- to late summer
Eryngium alpinum	75 (30)	5	Early to late summer
Eryngium bourgatii	45 (18)	6	Early to late summer
Eryngium tripartitum	100 (40)	5	Mid-summer to early autumn
Eryngium variifolium	60 (24)	5	Mid-summer to early autumn

Name	Height in cm (in)		No per m² (sq yd)	Flowering period
Erythronium 'Pagoda'	15	(6)	8	Mid- to late spring
Eupatorium purpureum 'Atropurpureum'	150–180	(60–72)	3	Late summer to mid-autumn
Euphorbia epithymoides	45	(18)	5	Mid- to late spring
Euphorbia griffithii 'Fireglow'	75	(30)	5	Early summer
Euphorbia sikkimensis	120	(48)	4	Early to mid-summer
Festuca glauca	25	(10)	5	—
Filipendula hexapetala 'Grandiflora'	75	(30)	5	Early to late summer
Gaillardia varieties	90	(36)	5	Early to late summer
Galega officinalis 'Her Majesty'	100–150	(40–60)	3	Early to mid-summer
Gentiana asclepiadea	60	(24)	5	Mid-summer to early autumn
Geranium endressii varieties	60	(24)	4	Early summer to early autumn
Geranium macrorrhizum 'Album'	30	(12)	5	Late spring to mid-summer
Geranium sanguineum	30	(12)	4–5	Early to late summer
Geum × *borisii*	30	(12)	5	Early summer
Geum chiloense varieties	60	(24)	5	Early to late summer
Gypsophila paniculata varieties	90	(36)	3	Early summer to early autumn
Helenium hybrids, tall	100–105	(40–42)	5	Mid-summer to early autumn
dwarf	90	(36)	5	
Helianthus multiflorus varieties	150	(60)	4	Mid-summer to early autumn
Helictotrichon sempervirens	60	(24)	3–4	Mid- to late summer
Heliopsis patula	150	(60)	4–5	Mid- to late summer
Helleborus niger	30	(12)	5	Early winter to early spring

Name	Height in cm (in)		No per m² (sq yd)	Flowering period
Helleborus orientalis	45	(18)	4	Late winter to mid-spring
Hemerocallis varieties	60–90	(24–36)	4	Mid-summer to early autumn
Heuchera varieties	60–75	(24–30)	5	Late spring to mid-summer
× *Heucherella tiarelloides*	30	(12)	4–5	Mid-spring to early summer
Hosta species and varieties	30–90	(12–36)	3–5	Mid-summer to early autumn
Inula 'Golden Beauty'	60	(24)	5	Early to late summer
Iris foetidissima	60	(24)	5	Early summer and autumn
Iris germanica varieties				
tall	90–120	(36–48)	5	Early summer
dwarf	30	(12)	7	Mid- to late spring
Iris pallida 'Variegata'	60	(24)	5	Early summer
Iris unguicularis	30	(12)	5	Mid-winter to early spring
Kniphofia caulescens	120	(48)	4	Autumn
Kniphofia hybrids	75–120	(30–48)	4	Mid-summer to mid-autumn
Lamiastrum luteum 'Variegatum'	25	(10)	4	Late spring to early summer
Lamium maculatum varieties	15–30	(6 – 12)	3 – 4	Mid-spring to early summer
Liatris 'Kobold'	60	(24)	5	Mid-summer to early autumn
Liatris spicata	60	(24)	5	Late summer and autumn
Limonium latifolium 'Violetta'	60	(24)	4	Mid-summer to early autumn
Linum narbonnense	45	(18)	5	Early summer to early autumn
Liriope muscari	30	(12)	5	Late summer to mid-autumn
Lupinus hybrids	100	(40)	4	Early to mid-summer

Name	Height in cm (in)	No per m² (sq yd)	Flowering period
Lychnis chalcedonica	100 (40)	5	Early to late summer
Lychnis coronaria varieties	60 (24)	5	Early summer to early autumn
Lychnis viscaria 'Splendens Plena'	30 (12)	5	Early to mid-summer
Lysimachia clethroides	100 (40)	4	Early autumn
Lysimachia punctata	90 (36)	4	Early to late summer
Lythrum salicaria varieties	75–90 (30–36)	4	Mid-summer to early autumn
Lythrum virgatum 'The Rocket'	90 (36)	4	Mid-summer to early autumn
Macleaya cordata	180 (72)	3	Late summer to early autumn
Meconopsis betonicifolia	90 (36)	5	Late spring to mid-summer
Meconopsis grandis	100 (40)	5	Late spring to early summer
Meconopsis × *sheldonii* 'Branklyn'	100 (40)	5	Late spring to mid-summer
Mertensia echioides	15 (6)	6	Early summer
Milium effusum 'Aureum'	60 (24)	5	Summer
Miscanthus sinensis 'Zebrinus'	200 (80)	4	Mid-autumn
Monarda didyma varieties	90 (36)	4–5	Early to late summer
Morina longifolia	75 (30)	5	Early summer to early autumn
Nepeta mussinii	30 (12)	5	Late spring to early autumn
Nepeta nervosa	15 (6)	5	Early to late summer
Oenothera glaber	45 (18)	5	Early summer to early autumn
Oenothera 'Highlight'	60 (24)	5	Early to late summer
Omphalodes verna	15 (6)	4	Early to late spring

Name	Height in cm (in)		No per m² (sq yd)	Flowering period
Ophiopogon planiscapus nigrescens	15	(6)	5	—
Paeonia lactiflora varieties	90	(36)	3	Early to mid-summer
Papaver orientale varieties	75–100	(30–40)	4–5	Late spring and early summer
Penstemon varieties	60–75	(24–30)	5	Early summer to mid-autumn
Phalaris arundinacea 'Picta'	60	(24)	3	Summer
Phlomis viscosa	100	(40)	4	Early to mid-summer
Phlox paniculata varieties				
tall	90	(36)	4–5	Mid-summer to
dwarf	60	(24)	4–5	early autumn

Here one is quite literally led up the garden path, which is charmingly bordered by an interesting collection of garden pinks.

Name	Height in cm (in)	No per m² (sq yd)	Flowering period
Phormium cookianum 'Cream Delight'	100 (40)	1	—
Phormium tenax dwarf varieties	60–90 (24–36)	1	—
Phormium tenax 'Purpureum'	200 (80)	1	—
Phygelius aequalis 'Yellow Trumpet'	60–75 (24–30)	4	Mid-summer to mid-autumn
Phygelius capensis	90 (36)	4	Mid-summer to mid-autumn
Phyllitis scolopendrium	45 (18)	4	—
Physalis franchetii	75 (30)	4	Early to late autumn
Physostegia virginiana	75–90 (30–36)	4	Mid-summer to early autumn
Polemonium foliosissimum	75 (30)	5	Late spring to late summer
Polygonatum multiflorum	75 (30)	5	Late spring to early summer
Polygonum affine	15–25 (6–10)	4	Early summer to early autumn
Polygonum bistorta 'Superbum'	90 (36)	3–4	Late spring to late summer
Polystichum setiferum	100 (40)	3	—
Potentilla hybrids	30–40 (12–15)	5	Early to late summer
Primula, primrose types	10–15 (4–6)	6–7	Early to late spring
Primula species, e.g. candelabra types	30–75 (12–30)	5	Late spring to mid-summer
Prunella grandiflora (syn. *P. webbiana*)	25 (10)	5	Early to mid-summer
Pulmonaria angustifolia	25 (10)	5	Mid-spring
Pulmonaria saccharata varieties	25 (10)	5	Early to late spring
Pyrethrum varieties	60–75 (24–30)	4	Late spring to mid-summer
Ranunculus gramineus	30 (12)	6	Late spring to mid-summer
Rodgersia pinnata varieties	90 (36)	3–4	Mid- to late summer

Name	Height in cm (in)	No per m² (sq yd)	Flowering period
Rudbeckia deamii	90 (36)	4–5	Mid-summer to early autumn
Rudbeckia fulgida 'Goldsturm'	75 (30)	5	Mid-summer to mid-autumn
Salvia superba varieties	45–75 (18–30)	5	Early summer to early autumn
Saxifraga × *urbium*	30 (12)	4	Late spring to early summer
Scabiosa caucasica varieties	75 (30)	5	Early summer to early autumn
Sedum aizoon 'Aurantiacum'	30 (12)	5	Mid- to late summer
Sedum 'Autumn Joy'	60 (24)	4	Late summer to mid-autumn
Sedum spectabile varieties	45–60 (18–24)	5	Late summer to mid-autumn
Sedum telephium 'Munstead Red'	45 (18)	5	Late summer to early autumn
Sidalcea varieties	90–100 (36–40)	5	Early to late summer
Smilacina racemosa	90 (36)	5	Mid- to late spring
Solidago varieties, tall	75–90 (30–36)	5	Late summer to early autumn
dwarf	30–45 (12–18)	5	
Stachys lanata 'Silver Carpet'	15 (6)	4	—
Stachys macrantha 'Superba'	60 (24)	5	Early to late summer
Stokesia laevis	30–45 (12–18)	5	Late summer to mid-autumn
Symphytum grandiflorum	25 (10)	5	Mid- to late spring
Symphytum rubrum	30 (12)	4–5	Late spring to mid-summer
Thalictrum dipterocarpum 'Hewitt's Double'	90 (36)	5	Mid- to late summer
Tradescantia virginiana varieties	45 (18)	5	Early summer to early autumn
Trillium grandiflorum	30 (12)	7	Mid- to late spring
Trollius × *cultorum* varieties	60–75 (24–30)	5	Late spring to early summer

Name	Height in cm (in)	No per m² (sq yd)	Flowering period
Verbascum 'Gainsborough'	120 (48)	5	Early to late summer
Verbascum hybrids, tall	100–120 (40–48)	5	Early to late summer
Veronica gentianoides	60 (24)	4	Mid-spring to early summer
Veronica spicata	45 (18)	5	Early summer to early autumn
Veronica teucrium	20–30 (8–12)	5	Early to late summer
Viola species and varieties	10–15 (4–6)	5–6	Mid-spring to late summer
Zauschneria californica	45 (18)	5	Late summer to mid-autumn
Zauschneria cana	45 (18)	5	Late summer to mid-autumn

The narrow border fronting this rose- and clematis-clad cottage is crammed with roses, lavender and catmint and edged with aubrieta, saxifrage and corydalis.

SUPPLIERS OF BORDER PLANTS

Beth Chatto
White Barn House
Elmstead Market
Colchester
Essex C07 7DB

Bressingham Gardens
Bressingham
Diss
Norfolk IP22 2AB

Hillier Nurseries (Winchester) Ltd
Ampfield House
Ampfield
Romsey
Hampshire S05 9PA

Kelways Nurseries
Langport
Somerset TA10 9SL

Notcutts Nurseries Ltd
Woodbridge
Suffolk IP12 4AF

Ramparts Nursery
Bakers Lane
Colchester
Essex C04 5BB

INDEX